The Seriously Silly
Book of
KIDS' JOKES

ARCTURUS

ARCTURUS

This edition published in 2014 by Arcturus Publishing Limited
26/27 Bickels Yard, 151–153 Bermondsey Street,
London SE1 3HA

ISBN: 978-1-78404-295-0
CH004305NT
Supplier 29, Date 0614, Print Run 3494

Written by Sean Connolly & Kay Barnham
Illustrations by Adam Clay & Dynamo Design
Designed by JMS Books
Edited by Joe Harris, Kate Overy & Joe Fullman

Printed in China

CONTENTS

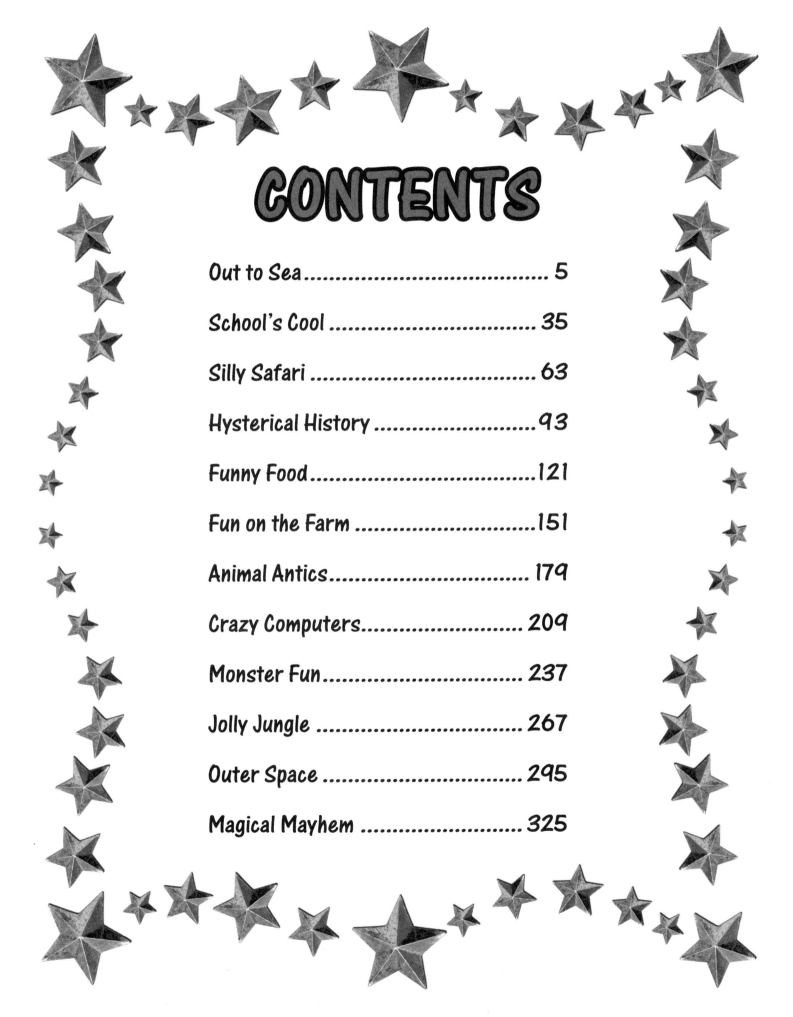

OUT TO SEA

Teacher: Where do you find starfish?
Pupil: In the Galack Sea!

What do sea captains tell their children at night?
Ferry tales.

Where do fish sleep?
On a waterbed!

Teacher: What musical instrument do Spanish
fishermen play?
Cast-a-nets!

Why don't clams give to charity?
Because they're shellfish.

Teacher: Why was no
one able to play cards
on Noah's Ark?
Pupil: Because Noah
stood on the deck!

What kind of noise makes
an oyster grouchy?
A noisy noise
annoys an oyster!

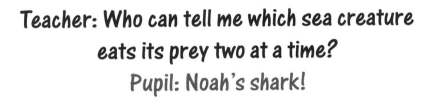

Teacher: Who can tell me which sea creature
eats its prey two at a time?
Pupil: Noah's shark!

Teacher: Why have you brought
that fish into school?
Pupil: Because we will be playing scales
in the music lesson!

Why are goldfish orange?
The water makes them rusty.

What lies at the
bottom of the ocean
and shakes?
A nervous wreck.

Customer: Waiter,
what's wrong with
this fish?
Waiter: Long time,
no sea.

What happened when the restless sleeper
bought himself a waterbed?
He got seasick.

Lifeguard: You can't fish on this stretch of beach!
Boy with fishing rod: I'm not – I'm teaching my
pet worm to swim.

What happened when the salmon went to Hollywood?
He became a starfish.

Why don't fish parents tell their children about electric eels?
They're just too shocking.

What music do they play in underwater nightclubs?
Sole music!

What game do fish like to play at parties?
Tide and seek.

What do you call a salmon wearing a suit and a tie?
So-fish-ticated.

Which fish once ruled Russia?
The tsar-dine.

Which two fish can you wear on your feet?
A sole and an eel.

Wife: Doctor, is there any hope for my husband?
He thinks he's a shipwreck.
Doctor: I'm afraid he's sunk, ma'am.

Why did the man go swimming in his
best clothes?
He thought he needed a wet suit.

Did you hear about
the two fish in a tank?
One was driving, and
the other was manning
the guns.

What did the
walrus do after
he read the
sad book?
He started
to blubber.

How can you tell that the ocean is feeling friendly?
It keeps waving at you.

How can you tell two octopuses are dating?
Because they walk along arm in arm in arm in arm
in arm in arm in arm in arm!

What can you expect from a clever crab?
Snappy answers!

How could you give yourself an injury gathering shellfish?
You might pull a mussel.

How do fish go into business?
They start on a small scale.

What book did the shark like reading best?
Huckleberry Fin!

Did you hear about the fisherman and the shepherd?
They got along by hook or by crook.

Why was the little iceberg just like his dad?
Because he was a chip off the cold block.

Why do whales sing?
Because they can't talk!

What do you call a gull that flies over a bay?
A bay-gull.

How do jellyfish police capture criminals?
In sting operations.

Why did the scuba diver hear
underwater singing?
He was in the Coral Sea.

How do you keep in touch with a fish?
You drop it a line.

How much sand would there be in a hole the
size of a truck?
None – holes are empty!

Where can you find an
ocean with no water?
On a map.

Why did Captain Hook
cross the road?
To get to the
secondhand store.

Where do ocean scientists keep their coffee mugs?
On the continental shelf.

Where do fish keep their savings?
In the river bank!

What do you call a man floating up and down on the sea?
Bob.

What happened when the boat carrying red paint
crashed into one carrying blue paint?
Both crews were marooned.

Who stole the soap from
the bathtub?
A robber duckie.

Why are dolphins smarter
than humans?
Because they can train
humans to stand
by the side of the pool
and throw them fish.

What song do they sing in the pig navy?
"Oinkers Aweigh".

Why didn't the sea captain's radio work in rough seas?
It was on the wrong wavelength.

What kind of fish are useful in cold weather?
Skates.

Which fish come out at night?
Starfish.

Why did the ship's captain look fed up?
He had a sinking feeling.

Why don't traffic lights ever go swimming?
They take too long to change.

Which sea creatures are the biggest cry babies?
Whales.

What did Santa say when he first spotted America?
"Land ho, ho, ho!"

How does an octopus go to war?
Well-armed.

Do undersea creatures play baseball?
Yes – there are 20,000 leagues under the sea.

What do pigs wear when they go swimming?
Hoggles.

**What's black,
incredibly rude,
and floats on water?**
Crude oil.

**What sort of hairstyle
do mermaids have?**
Wavy.

**Which movie do pirates
like to watch?**
Booty and the Beast.

What do British sea monsters eat?
Fish and ships!

What's fluffy and green?
A seasick poodle.

Why did the crab cross the road?
To get to the other tide.

Where is the safest place to see a man-eating fish?
In a seafood restaurant.

What grades did the pirate get in school?
High seas.

Which salad ingredient is the most dangerous
for ocean liners?
Iceberg lettuce.

Who held the baby octopus for ransom?
Squidnappers!

What's the best medicine for seasickness?
Vitamin sea.

What do you get if you cross a bad golfer
and an outboard motor?
I'm not sure, but I bet it goes,
"Putt, putt, putt, putt!"

Who wins all the money
at the undersea
poker games?
Card sharks.

What happens if you
cross an electric
eel with a sponge?
You get a shock
absorber.

Why did the shark do deep-sea diving?
Just for the halibut.

Why do pirates have a hard time learning the alphabet?
Because they spend so long at C.

How do you close an envelope underwater?
With a seal.

What sort of snacks can you buy on a Chinese boat?
Junk food!

What runs and runs without ever getting
out of breath?
A river.

How did Robinson Crusoe survive after
his ship sank?
He found some soap and washed
himself ashore.

Why wouldn't the sailor eat
any fruitcake?
He was worried about
dangerous currants.

What sort of boats do clever schoolchildren travel on?
Scholar-ships!

Which vegetables do pirates like best?
Aaaaartichokes.

What did the deep-sea diver
yell when he got caught
in seaweed?
"Kelp!"

What do you get if you meet a
shark in the Arctic Ocean?
Frostbite.

What do the underwater
police travel in?
Squid cars!

What did Cinderella wear
when she went skin diving?
Glass flippers.

Which sea creature can also fly?
A pilot whale.

Why did the pirate go into the computer store?
To buy an iPatch.

Why did the surfer wear a baseball glove?
Because he wanted to catch a wave.

What do you call a delinquent octopus?
A crazy, mixed-up squid!

Why did the sailor jump the rope?
He was the ship's skipper.

What do sailors like to do in their spare time?
Play water sports.

What did the ship say as it sailed into the port?
"What's up, dock?"

Why do fish in a school all swim in the same direction?
They're playing Salmon Says.

What did the shark plead in the murder case?
Not gill-ty.

How did the fisherman become rich?
He increased his net profits.

What did the pirate say when he got his
wooden leg caught in a freezer?
"Shiver me timbers".

What do sea monsters have for lunch?
A submarine sandwich.

What is in the middle of a jellyfish?
A jellybutton.

Where would you find a down-and-out octopus?
On squid row.

What do whales like to chew?
Blubber gum.

How do fish get to school?
By octobus.

**Why did the burglar
buy a surfboard?**
*He wanted to
start a crime wave!*

Who is the ocean's most dangerous outlaw?
Billy the Squid.

What did the fisherman say to the magician?
"Pick a cod, any cod."

What is the coldest animal in the sea?
The blue whale.

**What grouchy animal lives on the beach
and ignores everybody?**
A hermit crab.

Which fish works in a hospital?
A plastic sturgeon.

What's the best way to stuff a lobster?
Take it out for pizza and ice cream.

What do you call a baby squid?
A little squirt.

What position does the crab play on the baseball team?
He's the pinch hitter.

How is it that after a ship sank and every single person died, there were two people left?
They were married.

Are shellfish warm to touch?
No, they feel clammy.

How do you get a car unstuck in a mudflat?

With four-eel drive.

What happened when the tuna fisherman was caught stealing?

He got canned.

What happens to a green rock when you throw it into the Red Sea?

It gets wet.

What do you get when you graduate from scuba diving school?

A deep-loma.

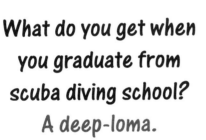

What do you call a massive mallard?

Moby Duck.

What do you get when you cross a bee with a seagull?
A beagle.

How does a penguin feel when it is left all alone?
Ice-olated.

What can you put into a barrel full of water
to make it lighter?
A hole.

What do pirates use
as kindling?
Fish sticks.

Why do sea lions
swim in salt water?
Because pepper
makes them
sneeze.

Which fish go to heaven
when they die?
Angelfish.

I'm on a seafood diet.
Are you losing weight?
No, because every time
I see food, I eat it.

Why did the bargain hunters
turn up at the marina?
They had heard about
the sails.

What are you likely to catch if
you use peanut butter as bait?
Jellyfish.

How did the dolphin make decisions?
It would flipper coin.

Which fish do knights like best?
A swordfish.

Who is the head of the underwater Mafia?
The codfather.

What kind of fish likes to eat between meals?
A snackerel.

What did the pirate say to the woman in the shoe store?
"Where's my booties?"

What did the passing seagull say to the pilot of the motorboat with no engine?
"How's it going?"

Are sharks fat?
No, they're just fin and bones.

Where do mermaids go to see movies?
The dive-in.

How does a boat show affection?
It hugs the shore.

What can fly underwater?
A mosquito in a submarine.

What do you use to cut the ocean in half?
A seasaw.

Which fish are the best at
home-improvement projects?
Hammerhead sharks.

Which part of a fish
weighs the most?
The scales!

What are net profits?
What fishermen have left
after paying the crew!

Teacher: What can you tell
me about the Dead Sea?
Pupil: I didn't even know
it was sick!

How do lighthouse keepers communicate
with each other?
With shine language.

Which beach item gets wetter the more it dries?
A towel.

What day do fish hate?
Fry day.

SCHOOL'S COOL

What did the dentist study at school?
Flossophy.

What did the number 0 say to the number 8?
"That's a cool belt."

Why did the teacher wear sunglasses?
Because his class was so bright.

Teacher: Did your dad help you with these questions?
Pupil: No, I got them wrong all by myself!

Why did the teacher jump into the swimming pool?
He wanted to test the water.

What kind of lunches do geometry teachers enjoy?
Square meals.

Why was the cross-eyed teacher's class rioting?
She couldn't control her pupils.

Why was the broom late for school?
It overswept.

Head: You will start with a basic salary but it will double in six months.
Teacher: In that case I think I would like to start in six months!

Teacher: Which of King Arthur's knights had the biggest horse?
Pupil: Was it Sir Eatalot?

Did you hear about the cannibal that
was expelled from school?
He was buttering up the teachers.

Teacher: What language do they speak in Cuba?
Pupil: Cubic!

Why did one pencil tell the other pencil
that it looked old and tired?
Because it was blunt.

What's the tastiest class at school?
History. It's full of dates.

My music teacher said I have a heavenly voice!
That's not strictly true – she said your voice was like nothing on Earth!

Teacher: You missed school yesterday, didn't you?
Pupil: Not very much!

Why did the pupil think the teacher had a crush on him?
She put "X"s all over his homework.

Teacher: Why are you taking that sponge into class?
Pupil: Because I find your classes so absorbing!

What is a polygon?
A dead parrot.

Why was the arithmetic textbook miserable?
It had too many problems.

What did the pencil say to the protractor?
Take me to your ruler.

Why was the music teacher locked out of his classroom?
The keys were on the piano.

English teacher: Give me an example of a long sentence.
Pupil: Life imprisonment.

I sprained my ankle and had to miss playing sport for 2 weeks.
Lucky you. Our sports teacher never accepts
a lame excuse for his class!

What do you get if you
cross a vampire and a
teacher?
Blood tests.

Why don't leopards bother
to cheat in exams?
Because they know
that they will always
be spotted!

Is the arithmetic teacher in
a good mood today?
I wouldn't count on it!

Teacher: Can you define
the word "hardship"
for me?
Pupil: Is it a boat made out
of concrete?

My French teacher is
a real peach!
You mean she's pretty?
No – I mean she has a heart
of stone!

What do history teachers do before they get married?
They go out on dates!

Science teacher: Why do doctors and nurses wear
masks in the hospital operating room?
Pupil: So if they make a mistake, no one will
know who did it!

Parent: Why have you given my son such a bad grade in his report? He's as intelligent as the next boy!

Teacher: Yes, but the next boy is an idiot!

Teacher: How did people spend their time in the Stone Age?

Pupil: Did they listen to rock music?

Parent: Do you think my son has what it takes to be a pilot?

Teacher: Well, he certainly spends plenty of time with his head in the clouds!

What happens when music teachers are sick?
They send in a note!

Why was the archaeology teacher unhappy?
Her career was in ruins.

History teacher: How would you discover
what life in Ancient Egypt was really like?
Pupil: I'd ask my mummy!

Did you hear about the
arithmetic teacher whose
mistakes started to multiply?
In the end, they had to take
him away!

Why does your teacher have
her hair in a bun?
Because she has a face like
a burger!

Why do nursery teachers have such a positive attitude?
They know how to make the little things count.

Parent: Do you think my son will make a good Arctic explorer?
Teacher: I would think so – most of his grades are below zero!

Teacher: Can you tell me what water is?
Pupil: It's a clear liquid that turns black when I put my hands in it!

Teacher: What is the plural of baby?
Pupil: Twins!

Why is that boy locked up in a cage in the corner of the classroom?
Oh, he's the teacher's pet!

I think our school must
be haunted.
Why?
Because the head teacher
keeps talking about the
school spirit!

Teacher: Who discovered
Pluto?
Pupil: Walt Disney!

Teacher: What do Attila the Hun and Winnie the Pooh
have in common?
Pupil: They have the same middle name!

Teacher: Michael, how do we know that the Earth
is round?
Michael: I didn't say it was, Mr Johnson!

Teacher: If you multiply 245 by 3,456 and divide the answer
by 165, then subtract 752, what will you get?
Pupil: The wrong answer!

Teacher: How good are you at picking up music?
Pupil: Well, I'm not sure if I could lift a whole piano!

Teacher: Jessica, how did you find the questions in your English test?
Jessica: Oh, I found the questions easily enough – it's the answers I couldn't find!

Teacher: Who invented fractions?
Pupil: Henry the Eighth!

Teacher: Please don't talk while you are doing your exam.
Pupil: It's all right, Miss Brown. We're not doing the exam – just talking!

Where do vampire schoolchildren go on school trips?
Lake Eerie!

How does an arithmetic teacher remove wax from his ears?
He works it out with a pencil!

Teacher: Why were you late this morning, Katie?
Katie: I squeezed the toothpaste too hard, and it took me
half an hour to get it all back into the tube again!

Pupil: Can we do some work on the Iron Age today?
Teacher: Well, I'm not certain, I'm a bit rusty on that period
of history!

Teacher: Ten cats were at
the cinema. One walked out.
How many were left?
Pupil: None – they were
all copycats!

Teacher: What's a
computer byte?
Pupil: I didn't even know
they had teeth!

Dad: Time to get up and go to school!
Son: I don't want to go! Everyone hates me and I get bullied!
Dad: But you have to go – you're the head teacher!

What happened after the wheel was first invented?
It caused a revolution!

Teacher: How many seconds are there in a year?
Pupil: Twelve – January 2nd, February 2nd...

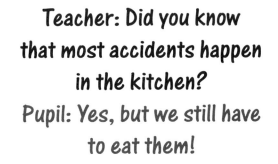

Teacher: Did you know
that most accidents happen
in the kitchen?
Pupil: Yes, but we still have
to eat them!

Science teacher: Fred, what
food do giraffes eat?
Pupil: Neck-tarines!

What did the music teacher
need a ladder for?
Reaching the high notes!

I banged my head on the classroom door this morning!
Have you seen the school nurse?
No, just stars!

Teacher: Why is your homework late?
Pupil: Sorry, Miss Elliot, my dad is a slow writer!

I'm not really interested in sums: I just go along to the lesson
to make up the numbers!

Teacher: How do archaeologists get into locked tombs?
Pupil: Do they use a skeleton key?

Teacher: In the future, all trains and buses
will run on time.
Pupil: Won't they run on fuel, just like now?

Did you hear about the PE teacher who used to run around the
classroom in order to jog pupils' memories?

What was the blackbird doing in the school library?
Looking for bookworms!

Why did the school orchestra have such awful manners?
Because it didn't know how to conduct itself!

Teacher: I wish you'd pay a little attention!
Pupil: I'm paying as little as I can!

Teacher: How did people react when electricity was first discovered?
Pupil: They got a nasty shock!

Teacher: I hope I don't catch you cheating in the spelling test!
Pupil: So do I, Miss Jones!

Which breed of dog do science teachers like best?
Labs!

When do 2 and 2 make more than 4?
When they make 22!

Sign outside the music department:
Violin for sale. Good price – no strings attached!

Teacher: Why was the invention of the
safety match an important change?
Pupil: It was a striking achievement!

Why did the school cafeteria hire a dentist?
To make more filling meals!

Parent: Do you think my son could work as a
DJ on the radio?
Teacher: He certainly has the face for it!

Why are teachers good at pool?
Because they always bring their own chalk!

How do you know your
school bus is old?
The seats are covered in
mammoth hide!

Why did the burglar break into the music department?
He was after the lute!

Did you hear about the arithmetic teacher and the art teacher who used to go out together?
They spent their time painting by numbers!

Why was Cinderella terrible at sports?
Because her coach was a pumpkin!

Teacher: This homework looks as though it has been written by your father.
Pupil: Of course it does – I borrowed his pen!

Teacher: Which two words in the English language have the most letters?
Pupil: Post Office!

Teacher: Where were all the kings and queens of France crowned?
Pupil: On the head!

Teacher: Which age did the mummies live in?
Pupil: The Band-Age!

What did the computer teacher name his baby son?
Chip.

Where did King Arthur's men get their training?
At knight school!

What sort of ring is always square?
A boxing ring!

Teacher: Eat up your school lunch – it's full of iron.
Pupil: That explains why it's so difficult to chew!

How many librarians does it take to change a lightbulb?
Two. One to screw it in and one to say, "Shhhhhh!" at the squeaking noise.

Book seen in the school library:
The Survivors' Guide to Escaping from a Sinking Ship
by Mandy Lifeboats

What do you say to the school's best pole vaulter?
Hiya!

Geography teacher: Where is the English Channel?
Pupil: I don't know, my TV doesn't have that one!

Why did the silly pupil buy a seahorse?
Because he wanted to play water polo!

Where do you find a giant scholar?
Around the neck of a giant's shirt.

Parent: Why didn't you come straight home from school?
Daughter: Because we live around the corner!

In a family with seven children, why was the youngest
late for school?
The alarm was set for six.

Why is 6 afraid of 7?
Because 7 ate 9!

Which tables don't they teach
you at school?
Dinner tables.

History teacher: Which
famous knight never won a
single battle?
Pupil: Sir Endor!

Teacher: What was Robin Hood's mother called?
Pupil: Mother Hood.

Teacher: What is the plural of mouse?
Pupil: Mice!
Teacher: And what is the plural of house?
Pupil: Hice!

Teacher: What is a myth?
Pupil: A female moth!

What's the difference between a train and a teacher?
A train says, "Choo choo!" but a teacher says, "Take that gum out of your mouth this instant!"

What were the 16 schoolboys playing in the telephone box?
Squash!

Teacher: Our school cafeteria is spotlessly clean.
Pupil: Is that why the food always tastes of soap?

Teacher: How do you make a sick insect better?
Pupil: Give it a T, then it will be a stick insect!

Geography teacher: Jack, where is Turkey?
Jack: No idea, sir, I haven't seen it since Christmas!

Music teacher: What sort of music can you make with your feet?
Pupil: Sole music!

Why did the school cook become a history teacher?
She was an expert on ancient grease!

Why did the French teacher have just one egg for breakfast?
Because he realized that un oeuf is enough!

Well, son, how did you find your geography test?
With a map and compass – how else!

Teacher: I think you need glasses.
Pupil: What makes you think that, Mr Adams?
Teacher: You're facing the wrong way!

Today is flying saucer day at the school cafeteria.
How come?
Because we get unidentified frying objects!

What do arithmetic teachers like eating?
Apple pi.

English teacher: For tonight's homework I want you to write an essay on Moby Dick.
Pupil: I can't do that, Miss Schneider!
Teacher: Why on earth not?
Pupil: I don't have any waterproof ink!

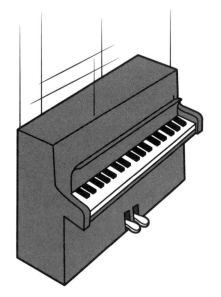

Teacher: If I gave you six coins per week for the next six months what would you have?
Pupil: A crazy teacher!

Why did the cyclops have to retire from teaching?
He only had one pupil!

Music teacher: What do you get if you drop a piano down a mineshaft?
Pupil: A flat minor!

History teacher: Why was the guillotine invented?
Pupil: As a cure for dandruff?

Teacher: In this exam you will be allowed 15 minutes for each question.
Pupil: How long do we get for the answers?

Why did the flea get expelled from flea school?
He just wasn't up to scratch!

Science teacher: Harry, how would you fix a short circuit?
Harry: Add some more wire to make it longer?

Teacher: Why were you late for school today?
Pupil: I got a puncture on my bicycle.
Teacher: Did you run over some broken glass?
Pupil: No, there was a fork in the road!

I've always had a hard time with decimals –
I just can't see the point!

Teacher: Where is the easiest place to find diamonds?
Pupil: In a deck of cards!

Pupil: I don't think I deserved a zero in this test.
Teacher: I agree – but it's the lowest mark I could
give you!

Teacher: Why are you doing your multiplication
on the floor?
Pupil: You told me not to use tables.

How did the school orchestra
leader survive being hit
by lightning?
He was a very bad
conductor!

SiLLY SAFARi

What's big, furry, and flies?
A hot-air baboon.

Where do reindeer run around and around in circles?
In Lapland.

What side of a porcupine is the sharpest?
The outside.

Why did the lion spit out the clown?
Because he tasted funny.

What did the tiger
eat after he'd had all his
teeth pulled out?
The dentist.

What do you call a
sheep with no legs?
A cloud.

Why do giraffes have
such long necks?
Because they have very
smelly feet.

What do you get if you cross a mole with an elephant?
Very big holes in the ground.

What's black and white and red all over?
A sunburned penguin!

Why do insects hum?
Because they can never remember the words!

What does an octopus
wear in the winter?
A coat of arms.

What do you call an
elephant in a phone box?
Stuck.

Where do sharks
come from?
Finland.

What's the difference
between a fish and
a piano?
You can't tuna fish!

Where are elephants found?
They're so huge, it's quite difficult to lose them
in the first place.

What's the best way to catch a fish?
Get someone to throw it at you.

What do you get if you cross a crocodile
with a camera?
A snapshot!

Why wasn't the girl scared when a shark
swam past her?
She'd been told it was a man-eater.

What kind of a wig has excellent hearing?
An earwig.

What game do elephants like playing best?
Squash.

A police officer saw a man walking down the street
with a penguin. He stopped the man and told him to take
the penguin to the zoo.
"Good idea," said the man, and off he went.
The next day, the police officer saw the man again.
He still had the penguin with him.
"I told you to take that penguin to the zoo,"
the police officer said.
"I did," the man replied. "He really enjoyed it,
so today I'm taking him to the cinema."

What has big ears, four legs, and a trunk?
A mouse going on vacation.

What did the shortsighted porcupine say to the cactus?
"Ah, there you are, dad!"

Spotted in the library: *I Fell Down a Rabbit Hole* by Alison Wonderland.

What is the best thing to do when a hippo sneezes?
Get out of the way!

What do you call a dead skunk?
Ex-stinked!

Why was the mother firefly sad?
Because her children weren't very bright!

What do penguins do in their spare time?
They chill.

What lives in a
forest and tells the dullest
stories ever heard?
A wild boar!

What did the silliest
kid in school call
his pet zebra?
"Spot!"

What would you do
if a jellyfish stung you?
I'd break every bone
in its body!

What does a frog use to put up shelves?
A toad's tool!

How did the fruit bats go into Noah's Ark?
In pears!

What do you call a criminal bird?
An illegal eagle!

Why are hyenas always arguing?
They always have a bone to pick
with each other!

What are the scariest dinosaurs?
Terror dactyls!

What sort of fish would you find in a bird cage?
A perch!

What sort of horses do monsters ride?
Night mares!

Which animal is the best rapper?
The hip-hop-opotamus!

Why does a cow moo?
Because its horns don't work.

What do you call a lion with chickenpox?
A dotted lion.

Did you hear about the brown bear who tripped
and fell into a blender?
It was a grizzly accident.

What is a big game hunter?
Someone who can't find the
soccer stadium!

Why can you never trick
a snake?
Because you can't pull
his leg!

HIPOPOP
HOPOTIP

Why did cavemen paint pictures of rhinoceroses
and hippopotamuses?
Because they couldn't spell their names!

Where do penguins vote?
At the South Poll.

Why are snails' shells so shiny?
They use snail varnish.

Where do giraffes go to be taught?
High school.

Why was the zebra put in charge of the jungle army?
Because he had the most stripes!

What's big, hairy, and always in a bad mood?
A Grrr-illa

How do you stop moles from digging up your lawn?
Hide the shovels.

What's the difference between a crazy rabbit
and a counterfeit bank note?
One's a mad bunny and the other's bad money.

What sea creatures do you find on
legal documents?
Seals.

Why should you never trust a whale with your
deepest, darkest secrets?
Because they're all blubbermouths.

Where do camels keep their money?
In sand banks.

Where do tadpoles change
into frogs?
In a croakroom.

What sort of animal will
never oversleep?
A llama clock!

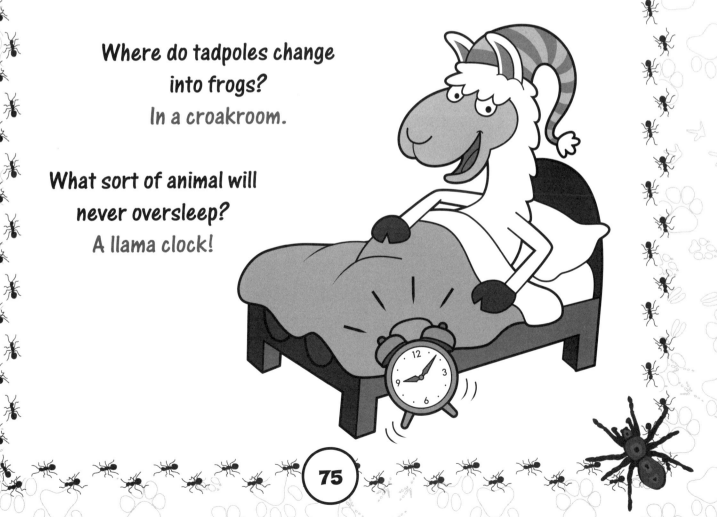

What do rhinos have that no other animal has?
Baby rhinos.

What do you get if you cross an angry
sheep with a cross cow?
An animal that's in a baaaaaaaaaaaaaaaad
moooooooooooooood.

Why can't leopards hide from hunters?
Because they are always spotted!

What job did the
spider get?
Web designer!

When do kangaroos
propose marriage?
In leap years!

Where do rabbits
learn to fly?
In the Hare Force!

Did you hear about the spiders who got married?
They had a huge webbing.

What do you call a worm in a fur coat?
A caterpillar!

What do you call a bad-tempered insect?
A grumblebee.

Doctor, I think I'm a frog.
So what's the problem?
I'm sure I'm going to croak.

What do you get if you cross a dinosaur with a fish?
Jurassic shark!

What do you call a telephone for alligators?
A croco-dial!

Did you hear about the wizard who made honey?
He was a spelling bee!

What do you call pigs who write to each other?
Pen pals!

How do elephants travel?
In jumbo jets!

What do camels wear when they play hide-and-seek?
Camel-flage.

What TV show do dolphin's like best?
Whale of Fortune.

What do you get if you cross a sheep with
a bucket of water?
A wet blanket.

What did the rabbit say when it went bald?
Hare today, gone tomorrow!

What do you call a giraffe
with one leg?
Eileen.

Which bird is always out
of breath?
A puffin.

Why do sick crabs walk sideways?
Because their medicine has side-effects!

What do you call a man who delivers Christmas
presents to lions and tigers?
Santa Claws!

How do you stop a skunk from smelling?
Hold his nose!

How can you tell if there's an elephant in the fridge?
You can't shut the door!

Why did the elephant
refuse to play cards with
his two friends?
Because one of them
was lion and the other
was a cheetah!

What do you call an
owl that robs the rich
and gives to the poor?
Robin Hoot!

What do toads say
when they greet
each other?
"Wart's new with you?"

What kind of pasta do goats like to eat?
Alpha-butt spaghetti!

What do you get if you cross a leopard and
a bunch of flowers?
A beauty spot!

Doctor, I think I'm a crocodile!
Don't worry – you'll soon snap out of it!

What do you give a deaf fish?
A herring aid.

How do you get
around on the seabed?
By taxi-crab!

What went into the lion's
cage at the zoo and came
out without a scratch?
Another lion!

Why was the mother
flea depressed?
All her children had gone
to the dogs!

How do you know if there's an elephant
in your fridge?
Look for footprints in the butter!

What did the blue whale say when he crashed into
the bottlenose dolphin?
"I didn't do it on porpoise."

How do you stop a rhino from charging?
Take away its credit card.

What happened to the shark that swallowed
a bunch of keys?
He got lockjaw!

Which animal was out of bounds?
The exhausted kangaroo.

What do you call a hippo
at the South Pole?
Lost!

What do you get if you cross a snake with a builder?
A boa constructor.

Where does a blackbird go for a drink?
To a crowbar.

What do porcupines say when they hug?
"Ouch!"

What do you get if you cross a fish with an elephant?
Swimming trunks.

What do horses wear at the beach?
Clip clops.

What do you call a monkey who is king of the jungle?
Henry the Ape!

What do you call an
85-year-old ant?
An antique!

Why do rabbits have
fur coats?
Because they'd look silly
in leather jackets.

Teacher: Billy, what
is a wombat?
Pupil: It's what you use
to play "wom", Miss!

Why did the hyena do so badly at school?
He thought everything was a joke.

How do you get down from a camel?
You don't. You get down from a goose.

What do you call a sleeping T. rex?
A dinosnore.

Who do fish borrow
money from?
A loan shark.

Knock knock!
Who's there?
Orang.
Orang who?
Orang the doorbell
but no one answered,
so now I'm knocking!

What has fifty legs?
Half a centipede!

On the school field trip a crab bit my toe!
Which one?
I don't know, all crabs look the same to me!

What made the fly fly?
The spider spied her.

What happened when the frog's car broke down?
It was toad away.

What happened when the elephant went
on a crash diet?
He wrecked four trucks, seven cars,
and a bus!

What do you call someone who lives with
a pack of wolves?
Wolfgang.

What do lizards
put on their
bathroom walls?
Rep-tiles.

Why are elephants
all wrinkly?
Have you ever tried
to iron one?

What did the celebrity squirrels sign before they
got married?
A pre-nutshell agreement.

Which newspaper do sheep prefer reading?
The Wool Street Journal.

What goes dash-dash-squeak, dash-dash-dash-squeak,
dot-dot-dash-squeak, dot-dot-dot-squeak, dot-squeak?
Mouse code.

What are the strongest creatures in the ocean?
Mussels.

**What kind of
of music do fish like?**
Bubble rap.

**Why did the fish
start miaowing?**
It was a catfish.

**What do you call a
parakeet that plays
ice hockey?**
A cheep skate.

Doctor, I keep thinking I'm a woodworm.
That must be so boring for you.

Why did the pig cross the road really, really slowly?
Because it was a road hog.

What's brown, furry, and has twelve paws?
The three bears.

What goes buzzzzzzzzz,
and loves to nibble cheese?
A mouse-quito!

First leopard: Hey, is that a
jogger over there?
Second leopard: Yes, great,
I love fast food!

What do you call a
shortsighted dinosaur?
Doyouthinkhesaurus.

Why are sharks so clever?
They are always fin-king.

What's black and white and black and white
and black and white?
A penguin rolling down a hill.

Why are fish easy to weigh?
They have their own scales.

What should you do if you see a blue whale?
Try to cheer him up.

Did you hear about the angry pig that lost its voice
from oinking too much?
It was disgruntled.

What do you call a woodpecker with no beak?
A headbanger!

How do dolphins make a decision?
They flipper coin.

What happened to the cannibal lion?
He had to swallow his pride.

What should you do if a rhino charges you?
Pay him!

What did the boa constrictor say to his girlfriend?
"I have a crush on you!"

What do you get if you cross a parrot with a shark?
A bird that will talk your ear off.

What did the bee say when it returned to the hive?
"Honey, I'm home."

HYSTERICAL HISTORY

When did early people start wearing uncreased clothes?
In the Iron Age!

What did Robin Hood wear to the Sherwood Forest ball?
A bow tie.

What sort of music did cavemen enjoy?
Rock music!

What was the moral of the story of Jonah and the whale?
You can't keep a good man down!

Teacher: Can you name a fierce warrior king?
Pupil: King Kong?

What was written on the knight's tomb?
"May he rust in peace."

Teacher: Name an ancient musical instrument.
Pupil: An Anglo-saxophone?

What should you do if you see a caveman?
Go inside and explore, man!

Why were undertakers in ancient Egypt such successful detectives?
They were good at wrapping up their cases.

What's purple and 5,000 miles long?
The grape wall of China.

Teacher: Surely you can remember what happened in 1776?

Pupil: It's all right for you – you were there!

Who was the fastest runner of all time?

Adam, because he was first in the human race!

Why did the king go to the dentist?

To get his teeth crowned.

Teacher: What were people wearing during the Great Fire of London?

Pupil: Blazers and smoking jackets!

Why was England so wet in the 19th century?

Because Queen Victoria's reign lasted 64 years.

Which ancient leader invented seasonings?
Sultan Pepper!

Who succeeded the first President of the United States?
The second one.

Why did the very first fries not taste very nice?
Because they were fried in ancient Greece!

Teacher: Can you name a famous religious warrior?
Pupil: Attila the Nun!

Teacher: Where would you find a cowboy?
Pupil: In a field – and stop calling me "boy!"

What type of music does an Egyptian mummy like best?
Wrap music!

How should you enter a room occupied by Henry VIII
and one of his wives?
Just amble in.

What do you call the king who invented the fireplace?
Alfred the Grate!

What did King Henry VIII do whenever he burped?
He issued a royal pardon.

Where was the Declaration
of Independence signed?
At the bottom.

Did prehistoric people
hunt bear?
No – they wore clothes!

How did Vikings send
secret messages?
By Norse code.

Which emperor should never have played with explosives?
Napoleon Blownapart!

Why do historians believe that Rome was built at night?
Because it wasn't built in a day.

In which battle was Alexander the Great killed?
His last one!

Why was George Washington buried at Mount Vernon?
Because he was dead.

What was King John's castle famous for?
Its knight life.

Which historical character was always eating?
Attila the Hungry!

What did Robin Hood say when he was almost hit at the archery tournament?
"That was an arrow escape!"

Teacher: Do you know the first President of the United States?
Pupil: No, we've never been introduced.

What did Attila's wife say to get his attention?
"Over here, Hun."

What did King George think of the American colonists?
He thought that they were revolting.

How do we know that the ancient Romans had
an expensive education?
Because they could all speak Latin.

What do Alexander the Great and Billy the Kid have
in common?
The same middle name.

Who would referee a tennis match between
Julius Caesar and Brutus?
A Roman umpire.

Which king had the largest crown?
The one with the biggest head!

Where did the Pilgrims land when they arrived in America?
On their feet.

In which era did people sunbathe the most?
The Bronzed Age.

What did the ancient Egyptians call bad leaders?
Un-Pharaohs.

Why did George Washington have trouble sleeping?
Because he couldn't lie.

Why did the T. rex wear a bandage?
He had a dino-sore!

Tour guide: When was the Magna Carta signed?

Mary: 1215.

Bill: Drat, we just missed it by half an hour!

Why did King Arthur have a Round Table?

So that no one could corner him.

Why does the Statue
of Liberty stand in New York?

Because it can't sit down.

Why did Eve move to
New York?

She fell for the Big Apple.

What was Noah's job?

He was an ark-itect.

Where do Egyptian mummies
go for a swim?

To the Dead Sea.

**What do you call
the Roman Emperor who
kept pet mice?**
Julius Cheeser!

**How did Moses cut
the sea in half?**
With a sea-saw.

**Teacher: How did
knights make
chain mail?**
Pupil: From steel wool?

What do you call an ancient joke?
Pre-hysterical!

Where were French traitors beheaded?
Just above the shoulders!

**What did King Arthur sleep with so he wouldn't get
scared of the dark?**
A knight light!

Which famous Roman ruler suffered from hay fever?
Julius Sneezer.

Teacher: Why did Robin Hood steal
from the rich?
Pupil: Because the poor didn't have anything
worth stealing!

Teacher: How did the Dark Ages get their name?
Pupil: Because there were so many knights!

First Roman soldier:
What's the time?
Second Roman soldier:
XV past VIII.
First Roman soldier:
By the time I work
that out, it will be
midnight!

How did the prince find the princess in the forest?
He followed the foot prince.

Why did Henry VIII have so many wives?
He liked to chop and change!

What do you call a pyramid overlooking the Nile?
A tomb with a view.

Which Italian explorer was best at aquatic sports?
Marco Water Polo.

Why did Columbus cross the ocean?
To get to the other tide.

Which Egyptian pharaoh played the trumpet?
Tootin' Kamun.

Which knight designed King Arthur's Round Table!
Sir Cumference!

What do history teachers talk about when they get together?
The good old days.

Why couldn't the mummy answer the phone?
He was too wrapped up!

Teacher: You know, an ancestor of mine came to this country by ship.
Pupil: Really? Which rat was he?

What was the first thing Queen Elizabeth I did when she ascended the throne?

She sat down.

Pupil: I wish I had been born 1,000 years ago.
Teacher: Why is that?
Pupil: Because I wouldn't have had to learn so much history!

How did the Roman cannibal feel about his mother-in-law?

Gladiator.

When did Ivan the Terrible die?

Just before they buried him!

What happened when the wheel was invented?

It caused a revolution.

How do you ask a dinosaur for a meal?

Tea, Rex?

What was the most popular movie in ancient Greece?

Troy Story.

Why did the student miss history class?

He had the wrong date.

Why did the pirate make a film?

Because he wanted to be a movie starrrrrrgh!

Where did Viking teachers send sick children?
To the school Norse.

Who sailed on the ghost ship?
The skeleton crew.

How was the Roman Empire cut in half?
With a pair of Caesars.

Which fruit launched a thousand ships?
Melon of Troy.

How did Vikings sleep on a longboat?
With their eyes shut.

What did the caveman give his girlfriend on Valentine's Day?
Ugs and kisses.

Why did the court jester swallow fire?
Because he wanted to burn some calories.

Did Adam and Eve ever have a date?
No, but they had an apple!

What did Julius Caesar say to Cleopatra?
Toga-ether we can rule the world!

Teacher: Today we're studying ancient Rome. Can anyone tell me what a forum was?
Pupil: A two-um plus a two-um?

Where did Napoleon keep his armies?
Up his sleevies.

What did Thomas Edison's mother say when he showed
her the electric light he had invented?
"That's wonderful, dear.
Now turn it off and go to bed."

Why did the Romans build straight roads?
So the soldiers didn't go around the bend.

Why did the nervous knight withdraw from
the archery contest?
It was an arrowing experience.

How did Robin Hood
tie his bootlaces?
With a long bow.

What happened
when electricity was
discovered?
Someone got a
nasty shock.

Why did the mammoth have a woolly coat? Because it would have looked silly in a parka.

Why did the archeologist go bankrupt? His career was in ruins.

Teacher: What came after the Stone Age and the Bronze Age? Pupil: The sausage?

What did Little John say to Robin Hood at the edge of the forest? I wooden go in there.

What has two eyes, two legs, and two noses?
Two pirates.

Why was Nefertiti convinced she didn't need a psychiatrist?
Because she was Queen of Denial.

Which historical figure entered the Olympic swimming
event without a bathing suit?
Lady Good-diver.

Who built the Ark?
I have Noah idea.

Why did King Arthur build
Camelot?
So he could park his camels.

PARKING

What did Columbus do after he crossed the Atlantic?
He dried his clothes.

What did Mount Vesuvius say to Pompeii?
I lava you.

Which protest by a group of cats and dogs took place in 1773?
The Boston Flea Party.

Why did Captain Cook sail to Australia?
It was too far to swim.

Why did Cleopatra take milk baths? She couldn't find a cow tall enough for her to take a shower.

If you cloned Henry IV, what would you get? Henry IV, Part II.

Which Viking explorer had a greenhouse on his longboat? Leaf Eriksson.

What do you call an archaeologist who sleeps all the time? Lazy bones.

What do you call George Washington's false teeth? Presi-dentures.

Why did the knight always carry a can opener? In case a bee flew into his helmet.

Why was Charlemagne able to draw such straight lines?
He was a good ruler.

What did Noah use to find his way in the dark?
Floodlights.

Are mummies covered in bandages?
Of corpse!

Why did the pioneers cross America in covered wagons?
Because they didn't want to wait thirty years
for the first train.

Which Native American tribe has always had the most lawyers?
The Sioux.

Why did the mammoth have a trunk?
Because it would have looked silly with suitcases.

Teacher: Can anyone tell me where Hadrian's Wall is?
Pupil: I think it's around Hadrian's backyard.

What happened to the knight who lost his left arm and left leg in battle?
He was all right in the end.

Which ancient Greek philosopher was the best swimmer?
Aris-turtle.

Where was the Ink-an Empire?
In Pen-sylvania.

What did the executioner say to the former king?
It's time to head off!

What did the cowboy say when he saw a cow in a tree?
Howdy get there?

Which of Queen Elizabeth's explorers tried to ride a bike
from England to America?
Sir Walter Raleigh.

Which pirate told the
most jokes?
Captain Kidd.

Who made dinner for Robin Hood and his
Merry Men?
Frier Tuck.

How does Moses make his tea?
Hebrews it.

What did people wear to the Boston Tea Party?
Tea-shirts.

FUNNY FOOD

Why did the cookie cry?
Because his mother had
been a wafer
so long.

When do truck drivers stop for a snack?
When they see a fork in the road.

What did one plate say to the other plate?
Lunch is on me.

**Why did the man eat yeast and furniture
polish for breakfast?**
He wanted to rise and shine.

Why did the apple go out with a pear?
Because he couldn't find a date.

This coffee is disgusting – it tastes like mud.
I'm not surprised – it was ground a few minutes ago!

Why did the chef serve frozen steak?
He wanted it to melt in the mouth.

What do you get if you cross a comedian and an orange?
Peels of laughter.

How did you like the restaurant on the Moon?
Not much, it lacked atmosphere.

What did the speedy tomato say to the slow tomato?
Ketchup!

Why did the bakers work late?
Because they kneaded the dough!

What cheese is made backward?
Edam!

Knock knock.
Who's there?
Cash.
Cash who?
No, thanks. I prefer walnuts.

Knock knock.
Who's there?
Arthur.
Arthur who?
Arthur any cakes left?

How do you make
a fruit punch?
Give it boxing lessons.

**Why did the girl stare
at the carton of
orange juice?**
Because it said
"concentrate" on
the label.

**Why was the chef
so relaxed?**
He had plenty of thyme
on his hands!

**What's yellow and
dangerous?**
Shark-infested custard.

Waiter, waiter – there's a fly in my soup!
Sorry, madam, I didn't know you were vegetarian!

**Did you hear about the turkey who tried to
escape the oven dish?**
He was foiled.

What do you get if you cross a Shakespeare play and an egg?
Omelet!

What did the fat man say when he sat down at the dinner table?
"Just think – all this food is going to waist!"

How do you make gold soup?
Put 14 carrots in it!

What do you call a lazy baker?
A loafer!

What do you get if you divide the circumference of a pumpkin by its diameter?
Pumpkin pi.

A pizza walks into a bar and asks for a lemonade.
'I'm sorry,' says the barman.
'We don't serve food.'

Chef: I didn't use a recipe for this casserole – I made it up out of my own head!
Customer: I thought it tasted of sawdust!

If I cut a potato in two, I have two halves. If I cut a potato in four, I have four quarters. What do I have if I cut a potato in sixteen?
Fries!

What did the pirate say to the cob?
Know any corny jokes?

Waiter, can I have my lunch on the patio?
Certainly, sir, but most people find a plate more sensible!

Why should you never tell secrets in a corn field?
Because there are ears everywhere!

What farm animal can you spread on toast?
A baby goat – it's a little butter!

What's the most expensive item on the menu at a Chinese restaurant?
Fortune cookies.

Mmmmm! This cake is lovely and warm!
It should be – the cat's been sitting on it all afternoon!

What do computer
operators eat for
a snack?
Chips!

How do they eat their
chips?
One byte at a time.

Which snack is wicked
and lives in the desert?
The sand witch!

How do you keep flies out of your kitchen?
Move the pile of rotting vegetables into the living room!

What starts and ends with "t" – and is also full of "t"?
A teapot.

What kind of bird is at every meal?
A swallow.

Why did the vampire
always carry a bottle of
tomato ketchup?
He was a vegetarian!

What is the one thing that
stays hot in the fridge?
Mustard!

What did the chewing gum
say to the shoe?
I'm stuck on you.

Why did the tomato turn red?
Because he saw the salad
dressing.

Knock knock.
Who's there?
Phil.
Phil who?
Phil this cup with sugar, would you, I've run out!

What do you get if you boil up 25 cars, three buses,
and a truckload of sugar?

Traffic jam.

Why is cutting a slice of gingerbread the easiest
job in the world?

It's a piece of cake.

Customer: Why is there a dead fly in my soup?

Waiter: Well, you surely don't expect to get a live one
at these prices!

What did one snowman say to the other snowman?

Can you smell carrots?

Why did the man send his alphabet soup back?
Because he couldn't find words to describe it!

Waiter – there's half a dead cockroach in my food!
You'll have to pay for the half you've eaten, sir!

How do you eat your turkey?
I just gobble it down!

Did you hear about the eggs who played
tricks on people?
They were practical yolkers.

Why do bees have icky,
sticky hair?
They use honeycombs.

Waiter – this crab only
has one claw!
Sorry, sir, it must have
been in a fight!
In that case, take it away and
bring me the winner.

What is the best time to pick apples?
When the farmer is away on vacation!

What do elves use to make sandwiches?
Shortbread!

Waiter, this pancake tastes awful!
Sir, I can assure you that our chef has been
making pancakes since he was a child!
That may be true, but can I have one of his
newer ones please?

Why did the lemon refuse to fight the orange?
Because it was yellow!

**There's a stick insect in my salad – fetch me
the branch manager at once!**

What did the carrot stick say to the tortilla chip?
"Want to go for a dip?"

Did you hear about the paranoid potatoes?
They kept their eyes peeled for danger.

Why are seagulls called seagulls?
Because if they flew over bays, they would
be bagels.

Did you hear about the farmer who took his cows
to the North Pole?
He thought he would get ice cream!

Doctor, I think I've just swallowed a chicken bone!
Are you choking?
No, I'm serious!

What sort of dog has no tail?
A hot dog!

What do garbage collectors eat?
Junk food.

Why couldn't Batman go fishing?
Because Robin had eaten all the worms.

Teacher: Philip, why
do you have a lunchbox in
each hand?
Pupil: It's important to
have a balanced diet,
Mr Harrison!

What do you get if
you mix birdseed with your
breakfast cereal?
Shredded tweet.

What is worse than finding
a worm in your apple?
Finding half a worm in
your apple!

What fast food do cannibals like best?
Pizza with everyone on it.

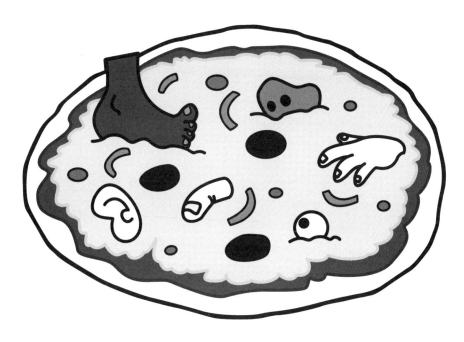

Did you hear about the strawberry who attended
charm school?
He became a real smoothie.

Knock knock.
Who's there?
Police.
Police who?
Police can I have a chocolate milkshake?

What do you call a pig that does karate?
A pork chop.

Why did the potato cry?
Its peelings were hurt.

How do you make a stiff drink?
Put cement in your cup.

What do you call a fake noodle?
An impasta.

Did you hear about Professor Cole, the scientist who discovered the perfect ratio for mixing cabbage, carrot, onion, and mayonnaise?
He called it Cole's Law.

What did one strawberry say to the other?
"Look at the jam we're in!"

Why did the boy throw the butter out of the window?
To see the butterfly!

What kind of nut always has a cold?
A cashew!

Why did the girl disappear into the bowl of muesli?
A strong currant pulled her under.

Johnny! How many more
times do I have to tell
you to keep away from
the cookie jar?
No more times –
it's empty!

What do you get if
you cross a chicken with
a cement mixer?
A bricklayer.

Why did the man wear a banana skin on each foot?
He wanted a pair of slippers.

Does Dracula's chef ever cook roast beef?
Yes, but very rarely.

What do dogs eat at the movies?
Pup-corn!

Knock knock.
Who's there?
Anita.
Anita who?
Anita nother hot dog – I'm starving!

How do you fix a broken pizza?
With tomato paste!

Why is a birthday cake like a golf ball?
They both get sliced.

Why are onions and beans dangerous?
Together they make tear gas.

Waiter, do you serve crabs?
Of course, sir. We serve anybody.

Our school lunches are untouched by human hand – there's a gorilla in the kitchen!

Where do hamburgers dance?
At meatballs.

What song does the saucepan like to sing?
"Home on the Range".

Why did the turkey cross the road?
It was the chicken's day off.

Why do bananas wear suntan lotion?
Because they peel!

What did the grape say when someone trod on it?
It let out a little whine.

What do you call a woman with a nut tree on her head?
Hazel.

Why did Mrs Grape leave Mr Grape?
Because she was tired of raisin kids.

Waiter! There's a fly in my soup!
Yes, sir, it's the bad meat that attracts them.

What are apricots?
Where baby
monkeys sleep.

We don't let Dad near the kitchen.
The last time he cooked, he burned the salad!

Waiter, will my pizza be long?
No, it will be round.

What do you call a cow with three legs?
Lean beef.

You can eat dirt cheap at the local diner!
Maybe so, but who wants to eat dirt?

What do you get from nervous cows?
Milkshakes!

What did one knife say to the other knife?

"Look sharp!"

Knock knock.

Who's there?

Wilma.

Wilma who?

Wilma lunch be ready soon?

Did you hear the joke about butter?

I'm not telling you – you might spread it.

What did baby corn say to her mother?

Where's popcorn?

What do you call stolen candy?

Hot chocolate.

What do you get
if you cross a turkey
with an octopus?
Eight drumsticks
for dinner.

Why did the man fill
his waterbed with
root beer?
Because he wanted
a foam mattress.

Waiter, this food isn't
fit for a pig.
I'm sorry sir; I'll bring you
some that is.

What do chimps wear when they're cooking?
Ape-rons!

Why are clocks greedy?
They always have seconds.

What is lemonade?
When you help an elderly lemon cross the road.

Waiter – this food is terrible. Bring me the manager.
I'm sorry, sir. He won't eat it either.

Waiter, there's a hand in my soup.
That's not your soup, sir, it's the finger bowl.

If it looks like a duck, walks like a duck, and talks like a duck... it probably needs a little more time in the oven.

Why shouldn't you tell an egg a joke?
Because it might crack up!

**Customer: Waiter, could you please tell me what
I've just eaten?**
Waiter: Why do you ask, sir?
Customer: Because I'll need to tell the doctor soon!

Which is the most musical fish?
The piano tuna.

**What did the octopus
hate about eating
every night?**
Washing his hands
before dinner.

**Where do the
toughest, meanest chickens
come from?**
From hard-boiled eggs.

What do you call a man
in a huge pot?
Stu.

If vegetarians eat
vegetables, does that mean
that humanitarians eat
humans?

Waiter, waiter, have you
smoked salmon?
No, sir, but I have smoked
a pipe.

What does a billionaire make for dinner every night?
Reservations.

Waiter – is there soup on the menu?
No, sir. I wiped it off.

Which part of Swiss cheese is the least fattening?
The holes!

What snack does a caveman like to eat?

A club sandwich.

Where is the best place to keep a pie?

Your tummy!

What did the golfer eat for lunch?

A sand wedge.

Knock knock.
Who's there?
Army.
Army who?
Army and you still going for ice cream?

What's the difference between a butcher and an insomniac?
One weighs a steak and the other stays awake.

FUN ON THE FARM

How do chicks get out of their shells?
They look for the eggs-it.

What's brown and sticky?
A stick!

What do you get it you cross a sheepdog and a fruit?
A melon-collie!

Teacher: Name five things that contain milk.
Pupil: Yogurt, cheese, and three cows!

What do you get when
you cross a rooster
with a duck?
A bird that gets
up at the
quack of
dawn.

What ballet is popular
with pigs?
Swine Lake.

Teacher: How would
you hire a farm worker?
Pupil: Put a brick
under each leg.

What did the pig say
when the farmer grabbed
him by the tail?
"That's the end of me."

Knock, knock!
Who's there?
Farmer.
Farmer who?
Farmer distance, your house looks much bigger!

What happened when the sheep pen broke?
The sheep had to use a pencil.

Knock, knock!
Who's there?
Lass.
Lass who?
How long have you been a cowboy?

What do you call a donkey
with three legs?
Wonky donkey.

How do you make a
chicken stew?
Keep it waiting for a
couple of hours.

Texan: On my uncle's
ranch, cowboys
round up cattle
on horseback!
New Yorker: Wow!
I didn't know cows could
ride horses!

What do you get if you
cross a cow with a
grass cutter?
A lawn mooer!

How do you make
an apple puff?
Chase it around
the kitchen.

Where do horses stay
in hotels?
The bridle suite.

What do you get if you cross a cow and a goat?
Butter from a butter!

Is chicken soup good for your health?
Not if you're the chicken!

What do you call a cow with no milk?
An udder failure

Did you hear about the scarecrow who won a gold medal?
He was out standing in his field.

What did the waiter say when the horse walked
into the café?
"Why the long face?"

What has lots of ears, but can't hear anything at all?
A cornfield.

What did the alien say to
the plant?
"Take me to your weeder."

What did the farmer
use to repair his
overalls?
A cabbage patch.

How did the banana know
he was sick?

He wasn't peeling well.

Patient: Doctor, I feel as sick as a dog!
Doctor: I'll make an appointment for you to
see a veterinarian!

Where do sheep go on their summer vacation?
The Baaahaaamaaas!

Patient: Doctor, I feel like a goat!
Doctor: Really? And how are the kids?

What's green and sings in the vegetable patch?
Elvis Parsley.

What did the horse say when it fell over?
"I've fallen and I can't giddy-up."

Knock, knock!
Who's there?
Lettuce.
Lettuce who?
Lettuce in and you'll find out!

Patient: Doctor, what can I do to help me get to sleep?
Doctor: Have you tried counting sheep?
Patient: Yes, but then I have to wake up to drive home again!

What do you give a sick pig?
Oinkment!

How did the musical farmer know which note to sing?
He used a pitchfork!

What do you call the wages paid to a gardener?
His celery!

What sort of jokes do chickens like best?
Corny ones!

What do you call a sleeping bull?
A bulldozer.

What do you get if you cross a chicken with a kangaroo?
Pouched eggs!

How did the pig with laryngitis feel?
Dis-gruntled.

Why do roosters curse all the time?
They are fowl-mouthed.

What do you call a car
full of eggs?
A hatchback.

What do you call a
dancing sheep?
A baalerina.

What did the chicken say
when it laid a square egg?
Owwww!

What did the flamenco-dancing farmer say to his chickens?
"Oh, lay!"

What do cows like to do at the weekend?
Go to the moovies.

What do cows eat for breakfast?
Moosli!

What do you get if you feed gunpowder to a chicken?
An egg-splosion!

Doctor, I feel like a dog!
How long have you felt that way?
Since I was a puppy!

What did the farmer use to paint the new sty?
Pigment.

What do you call a factual
TV show about sheep?
A flock-umentary!

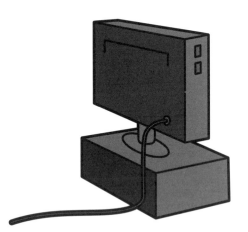

Why did the goose cross the road?
To prove she wasn't chicken!

Patient: Doctor, I got trampled by a load of cows!
Doctor: So I herd!

What do you give a pony with a cold?
Cough stirrup!

Why should you never tell your secrets to a piglet?
Because they might squeal!

How do alien farmers round up their sheep?
They use tractor beams!

What do you get when you cross a chicken and a fox?
Just the fox.

How can you cook turkey that really tickles
the taste buds?
Leave the feathers on!

Where do cows go for
history lessons?
To a mooseum!

How many pigs do you
need to make a smell?
A phew!

What do you call
a cow with an
out-of-date map?
Udderly lost!

Why did the pig run away from the farm?
He felt that the others were taking him for grunted.

What are bacon thieves called?
Pig-pockets!

Why was the butcher looking worried?
His job was at steak.

Two flies have landed
on the farmer's front porch.
Which one is the actor?
The one on the screen!

If a small duck is called
a duckling, what do you
call a small pen?
An inkling!

What do you get if you sit
under a cow?
A pat on the head.

What do you call a dog with a bunch of roses?
A collie-flower!

Why did the farmer's dog keep chasing his tail?
He was trying to make ends meet.

How does a sheep finish a letter?
Sincerely ewes.

Why did the chicken cross the playground?
To get to the other slide!

What do you get if
you cross a cow and
a jogging machine?
A milk shake!

What grows down
as it grows up?
A goose!

Why is that farmer
setting fire to the plants
in his field?
He's growing baked beans!

How many sheep does it take to make a wool sweater?
I didn't know sheep could knit!

What fairy tale is popular with pigs?
Slopping Beauty.

What do you call a man who keeps rabbits?
Warren!

What says, "Moo, baa, woof, quack, meow, oink?"
A sheep that speaks foreign languages!

What do you get if you cross a cow with a camel?
Lumpy milkshakes!

How do you stop a dog from barking in the front yard?
Put him in the back yard.

How does your dog get into the house?
Through the labra-door!

Why are bulls so noisy?
Because they each have two horns.

What do you call a tale with a twist at the end?
A pigtail!

How did the farmer feel when she lost her flashlight?
Delighted.

How do hens dance?
Chick to chick!

What kind of jewels do
vegetables wear?
Onion rings.

Why is it hard to carry
on a conversation
with a goat?
Because they're always
trying to butt in.

What do you call
a baby turkey?
A goblet.

What do you call a veterinarian with laryngitis?
A hoarse doctor.

What do penguins use to stay beautiful?
Cold cream.

Where do sheep get shorn?
At the baa-baas!

What does it mean if you find a set of horse shoes?
A horse is walking around in his socks!

Why did the boy stand behind the horse?
He thought he might get a kick out of it.

What do you get from a forgetful cow?
Milk of amnesia.

What steps should you take if you see a bull charging toward you?
Big steps, and fast!

What do you call a Russian gardener?
Ivanhoe!

What do ducks watch on TV every day?
The feather forecast.

Mother: You can't keep a pig in your bedroom – what about the terrible smell?
Child: Don't worry, he'll soon get used to it!

What do you get if you cross a sheep with a porcupine?
An animal that knits its own sweaters.

What do you get from a pampered cow?
Milk that's spoiled.

If you had fifteen cows and five goats, what would you have?
Plenty of milk!

Why did the chicken run out onto the basketball court?
Because the referee whistled for a fowl!

Young man, can you reach that package of beef
from the top of the freezer?
No ma'am. The steaks are too high.

How does a bull buy his food?
He charges it.

What did the polite sheep say to his
friend at the gate?
After ewe.

Can pigs fly?
No, but swine flu.

Why do pigs never go
on vacation?
They prefer to sty
at home.

What did the duck say
when she bought lipstick?
Put it on my bill!

Why did the two pigs go to Las Vegas for their vacation?
To play on the slop machines.

Why does Santa have three gardens?
So he can hoe hoe hoe.

What kind of dog hides in a pile of leaves?
A Jack Russell.

What do you call a duck with fangs?
Count Duckula.

What has five fingers and drives a tractor?
A farm hand.

What kind of animal goes OOM?
A cow walking backward!

What do you call cattle that tell each other jokes?
Laughing stock.

When do you know it's time for a farmer's family to go to sleep?
When it's pasture bedtime.

A cross between a cocker spaniel and a poodle is a called a cockapoo. So what do you call a cross between a cockapoo and a poodle?
A cock-a-doodle-do!

Why did the farmer prepare his field with a steamroller?
He wanted to grow mashed potatoes.

What day do eggs hate the most?
Fry-day.

Which horses aren't afraid
of the dark?
Nightmares.

What do you call a chicken
crossing the road?
Poultry in motion.

What is the best way to
carve wood?
Whittle by whittle.

Why do male deer need braces?
Because they have
buck teeth.

Why did the rooster get a tattoo?
He wanted to impress the chicks.

What do you get from an invisible cow?
Evaporated milk.

First cow in a field: Moo.
Second cow: Ohhh, I was going to say that!

Why did the ram run over the cliff?
He didn't see the ewe turn!

What happened when the owl lost her voice?
She didn't give a hoot.

What did the buffalo say to his son when
he went away?
Bison!

Why didn't the piglets listen to their father?
Because he was an old boar.

Why did the farmer
think someone was spying
on him?
There were moles all
over his field.

Which play is popular
with pigs?
Hamlet by
Shakespeare.

Why did the pterodactyl cross the road?
Because chickens didn't exist back then.

How do you save a drowning rodent?
Use mouse to mouse resuscitation.

What do you get when you cross a cow
with an octopus?
A cow that can milk itself.

ANIMAL ANTICS

Why are dogs such bad dancers?
They have two left feet.

What's worse than raining cats and dogs?
Hailing taxis.

What happened to the cat that swallowed a ball of wool?
She had mittens.

How can you keep a wet dog from smelling?
Hold its nose.

Hey, you can't fish here, this is a private lake!
I'm not fishing, I'm teaching my pet worm to swim!

Have you put some more water in the goldfish bowl?
No. It still hasn't drunk the water I put in when
I first bought it!

What happens when ducks tell each other jokes?
They quack up.

What's the special offer at the pet shop this week?
Buy one cat – get one flea!

What do you call a high-rise pigpen?
A styscraper.

First cat: Where do fleas
go in the winter?
Second cat: Search me!

Why did the dog wear
gloves?
Because it was a boxer.

My dog's a blacksmith.
How can you tell?
When I tell him off, he makes a bolt for the door.

Why did it take the Dalmatian so long to choose a vacation?
He was looking for just the right spot.

Why was the cat scared of the tree?
Because of its bark.

How did the puppy stop
the DVD player?
He used paws.

What animal wears a long
coat in the winter and pants
in the summer?
A dog!

What is a good pet for
small children?
A rattlesnake!

What type of dog can tell the time?
A watchdog.

How do you spell mouse trap using only 3 letters?
C.A.T!

Which pets are the noisiest?
Trumpets!

Why did the rabbit go to the doctor?
Because she felt jumpy.

What did the clean dog say to the dirty dog?
Long time no flea!

How do you stop a dog from barking in the
back seat of a car?

Put it in the front seat.

What are dog biscuits made from?

Collie-flour!

What is spotted, has whiskers, and jumps
every ten seconds?

A leopard with hiccups.

Why did the dog limp into the Wild West saloon?

He came to find the cowboy who shot his paw!

I think I'm turning into a young cat.
You must be kitten me!

What do you call a cat that chases outlaws?
A posse cat!

What do you get if you cross an insect and a rabbit?
Bugs Bunny.

Did you hear about the well-behaved cat?
It was purrfect.

Jimmy: My pet's called Tiny.
Katie: Why?
Jimmy: Because he's my newt.

Knock, knock!
Who's there?
Alf.
Alf who?
Alf feed the cat while you're away!

What do you call a column topped with
a statue of a famous feline?
A caterpillar!

Why do pigs make
terrible drivers?
They're all road hogs.

What did the dog say
when it sat on some
sandpaper?
"Ruff!"

What do you call a cat
with eight legs?
An octopuss.

What do you call a woman
with a cat on her head?
Kitty.

What did the dog say
when his owner stopped
him from chewing the
newspaper?
"You took the words out
of my mouth!"

What do you get if you drop
birdseed in your shoes?
Pigeon toes.

Advert in a local paper:
"Dog free to good home – eats anything.
Loves children!"

My dog is a real problem. He chases anything and
everything on a bike. I don't know what to do.
Just take his bike away!

Which cats are great at bowling?
Alley cats.

What sort of dog is good at looking after children?
A baby setter.

Doctor, I think I'm a cat!
How long have you felt like this?
Since I was a kitten!

What do you get if a cat sits on a beach at Christmas?
Sandy claws!

What happened to the Scottish cat that
ran into the road without looking?
It was kilt!

How do you find a lost dog?
Make a sound like a bone!

Teacher: Can you define "dogmatic?"
Pupil: Is it a robot pet?

Did you hear about the cat that sucked a lemon?
He was a sourpuss.

What game do horses like playing?
Stable tennis.

What's the difference between a well-dressed
gentleman and an exhausted dog?
One wears an expensive suit and the
other just pants.

What kind of fish will help you to hear better?
A herring aid.

Dad: Did you put the cat out?
Kid: I didn't need to. It wasn't on fire!

What do you use to
clean a cat's hair?
A catacomb.

What do you give
a sick parakeet?
Tweetment!

Why was the pig covered in ink?
Because it lived in a pen.

How do you make a cat happy?
Send it to the Canary Islands!

What time is it when a moose sits in your canoe?
Time to get a new canoe.

What do you call a dog that is always
rushing around?
A dash-hound!

Where do you buy
baby birds?
At the chickout.

Where do rabbits
go to buy
their clothes?
The hopping mall.

What does your pet snake
become if he gets
a government job?
A civil serpent!

Doctor, I think I'm a dog.
Well, take a seat and I'll have a look at you.
I can't – I'm not allowed on the furniture!

Did you hear about the boy who spilled spot remover
on his dog?
The dog vanished.

Why did the chicken sit on an axe?
She wanted to hatchet.

What did the parking attendant put on the car outside the dog kennel?
A barking ticket.

What is a popular hobby for dogs?
Flea collecting.

What kind of bears like to get wet in the rain?
Drizzly bears.

Why did the cat say "woof" to the dog?
It was speaking in a foreign language.

What do you get when you cross a parrot and a cat?
A carrot!

Where do huskies train for dogsled races?
In the mushroom.

Why did the dogs jump in the lake?
To catch a catfish.

What type of pet just lies around doing nothing?
A carpet.

Why did the monkey go to
sleep on the chandelier?
Because he was a
light sleeper.

What's the difference
between a buffalo
and a bison?
You can't wash in a buffalo!

What do you call a
prisoner's parakeet?
A jail bird!

Why did the cat
pounce on the
computer?
Because he saw
a mouse.

What's happening
when you hear
"Meow – splat!
Woof – splat!"
It's raining cats
and dogs.

Where do birds invest their money?
In the stork market.

Did you hear about the cat who drank three saucers
of water in one go?
She wanted to set a new lap record!

On which day do lions eat people?
Chewsday.

What did the cowboy say when the bear ate
his hunting hound?
Doggone!

What's red
and green and
jumps out of planes?
A parrot-trooper!

Why did the Dalmatian go
to the eye doctor?
He was seeing spots.

What did Shakespeare's
cat say?
"Tabby, or not tabby..."

Why do dogs run in circles?
Because it's hard to run in squares.

What do you use to comb a rabbit?
A hare-brush.

What do you get when you cross a dog with a sheep?
A sheep that can round itself up.

Why do dogs wag their tails?
Because no one else will do it for them.

What do ducks wear to the beach?
Beakinis.

What happens when cats fight?
They hiss and make up.

What do you call rabbits marching backward?
A receding hare-line.

Why do terriers make great fighter pilots?
Because they're good in a dogfight.

Why did the girl oil her pet mouse?
Because it squeaked.

What did the bunny say to the carrot?
It's been nice gnawing you.

What's more astounding than a talking dog?
A spelling bee.

What do you say to a dog before he eats?
"Bone appetit!"

What do you call a cat that does tricks?
A magic kit.

What do you call an Alsatian in jeans and a T-shirt?
A plain-clothes police dog.

What did the canary say when its new cage fell apart?
"Cheep! Cheep!"

What do you call a guard dog with a cold?
A germy shepherd.

How does a cat sing the musical scale?
Do-re-meow.

What do you call a hamster that can pick up an elephant?
Sir!

What does a cat say when he gets hurt?
Mee-OW!

What do you get when you cross a dog with an elephant?
A really nervous postman.

What do you get when you cross a parrot with a pig?
An animal that hogs the conversation.

What do cats use to make coffee?
A purr-colator.

What happens if you mix a bird, a car, and a dog?
A flying carpet.

What kind of cat keeps the grass short?
A lawn meower.

Cat bumper sticker:
"Life is hard – then you nap."

What kind of bird does construction work?
A crane.

Did you hear about the pig who walked around the world?

He was a globetrotter.

Why is it called a "litter" of puppies?

Because they mess up the whole house.

What do chickens keep beside their beds?

Alarm clucks.

What did one flea say to the other flea?

"Should we walk or take the dog?"

Which birds steal from
the bathroom?
Robber ducks.

Zookeeper: Why do pandas like watching really
old movies on television?
Tommy: Because they're all in black and white.

Which cat led the Chinese Revolution?
Chairman Meow.

What do lazy dogs do for fun?
They chase parked cars.

**Why did the tortoise
cross the road?**
To get to the
Shell garage.

Why do birds lay eggs?
Because if they dropped
them, they'd break.

**What's black and white and
goes round and round?**
A penguin in a
revolving door.

What do you call an unwashed elephant?
A smellyphant.

Where do young dogs sleep when they camp out?
In pup tents.

What do you say to a hitchhiking kangaroo?
Hop in!

When is it unlucky to see a white cat?

When you're a mouse.

How does a mouse feel after a shower?

Squeaky clean!

Who always succeeds?

A parakeet with no teeth.

Why was the toucan
kicked out of the hotel?
Because he had an
enormous bill!

What do you call a cat that has
just eaten a whole duck?
A duck-filled fatty puss!

Why are dogs longer at night than during the day?
Because they are let out in the evening and taken in
in the morning.

Why did the teenage pig have to tidy her room?
Because her parents said it looked like a pigsty.

Can a cat play patty-cake?
Paw-sibly.

What's it called when a dog does a TV commercial?
Ad-fur-tisement.

Which of Santa's reindeers has very bad manners?
Rude-olph.

What do you get if you cross a dog with
a cheetah?
A dog that chases cars – and catches them!

In which month do dogs bark the least?
In February – it's the shortest month!

How did the little Scottish dog feel when
he saw the monster?
Terrier-fied.

What do you get if you cross a donkey and Christmas?
Muletide greetings!

Why should you be careful where you step when it rains cats and dogs?
You could step in a poodle!

What was the result when two silkworms had a race?
It ended in a tie.

What do horses tell their children at bedtime?
Pony tales!

What do you call a Scottish parrot?
A macaw!

CRAZY COMPUTERS

Why did the robot leave school so young?
He was always being upgraded.

Where is the world's biggest computer?
In New York – it's the Big Apple!

Which cartoon character do robots like best?
Tintin!

Why did the medical computer go to prison?
It had performed an illegal operation.

Where does the biggest spider in the universe live?
On the World Wide Web.

What do you call a man with a speedometer in the middle of his forehead?
Miles!

How do computers say goodbye?
"See you later, calculator!"

Teacher: Steven, what's a computer byte?
Pupil: I didn't even know they had teeth!

Teacher: Can you give me an example of software?
Pupil: A wool sweater?

What do you get if you cross a computer with a lifeguard?
A screensaver.

Why are birds always
on the Internet?
They just love
tweeting.

What was the robot doing at the gym?
Pumping iron.

Why did the robot boxer sit on the stove before the
big match?
He wanted to strike while the iron was hot.

Which cookie do computers like best?
Chocolate microchip.

If human babies are delivered by stork, how are
robot babies delivered?
By crane!

What did the computer nerd say when he opened the curtains?
Wow, look at those graphics!

Why are evil robots so shiny?
Because there's no rust for the wicked.

Why did the computer need glasses?
To improve her web sight.

Spotted in the library:
Robots Are People Too by Anne Droid.

What happened to the robot who put his shoes on the wrong feet?
He had to be rebooted.

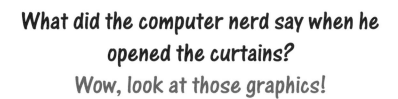

What's orange and points North?
A magnetic carrot.

First robot: Are you enjoying that book about magnetism?
Second robot: Yes, I can't put it down!

Why was the thirsty astronaut hanging out near
the computer keyboard?
He was looking for the space bar.

Did you hear about the
couple who adopted a
calculator?
It made a great addition
to the family.

Why did the Apple Mac
programmer live in
the dark?
Because he refused
to use Windows.

Why did the boy bring a
surfboard to school?
The teacher said they
were going to be surfing
the Internet.

Why was the computer
such a terrific golfer?
It had a hard drive.

How do lumberjacks
get on the Internet?
They log on.

What do you call a man with a cable coming out
of his ear?
Mike!

What do you buy for someone who already has all
the latest gadgets?
A burglar alarm.

**Why did the robot
get angry?**
Someone kept pushing
his buttons!

**What do you get if
you cross a large computer
and a hamburger?**
A Big Mac!

**Why do robots never
feel queasy?**
They have cast
iron stomachs.

Why did the pupil fall asleep in computer class?
He was feeling key-bored.

Jane: My computer's making a humming noise!
Tom: It must be a hum bug.

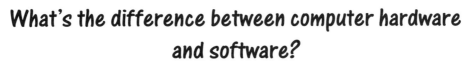

What's the difference between computer hardware and software?
Hardware is the stuff that you can kick when it doesn't work.

What goes in one year and out the other?
A time machine!

Teacher: Give me an example of cutting edge technology.
Pupil: A pair of scissors?

My computer is powered by clockwork.
Really?
No, I was just winding you up.

What type of music do robots like best?
Heavy metal!

How can you tell if a robot is happy to see you?

Because his eyes light up.

What do you get from robot sheep?

Steel wool.

Why did the computer programmer give up his job?

He lost his drive.

Why was the electrified robot so badly behaved?

It didn't know how to conduct itself.

Did you hear about the robot dog?

His megabark was worse than his megabyte.

What do you
call a robot who
turns into a tractor?
A trans-farmer!

Where do cool
mice live?
In mouse pads.

Did you know that
my computer can do
the gardening?
Can it really?
Yes, it's made
with cutting
hedge technology.

What is a baby computer's first word?
Data.

Did you hear about the two TVs who got married?
Their reception was excellent.

Why did the boy and girl robots call things off after their first date?
There was no spark.

Why did the robot kiss his girlfriend?
He just couldn't resistor.

Why did the storekeeper refuse to serve italic fonts?
He didn't like their type.

Where did the tightrope walker meet his girlfriend?
Online.

What do you call a flying printer?
An inkjet.

Which city has no people?
Electricity.

How do snowmen get online?
They use the Winternet.

Why should you not be upset if a computer beats you
at chess?
You can still beat it at table tennis.

Spotted in the library:
*How to Build a
Shrink Ray* by
Minnie Mize.

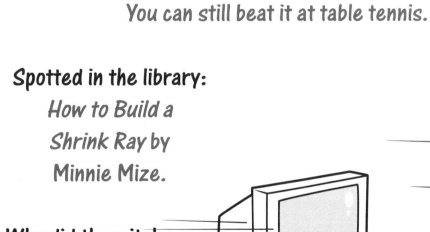

Why did the witch
buy a computer?
She needed a
spell-checker!

Why don't elephants use
computers?
Because they are scared
of the mouse!

Which superhero will
get the creases out
of your shirts?
Iron Man.

Why didn't the cheap
laptop work?
Because the battery was
given free of charge.

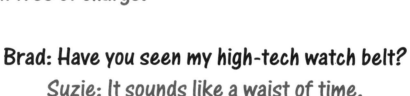

Brad: Have you seen my high-tech watch belt?
Suzie: It sounds like a waist of time.

What flies through the air and tastes great with
peanut butter?
A jelly-copter.

Why was the supercharged android so popular at parties?
He was a real live wire.

Doctor, I keep thinking I'm a computer.
Come into the hospital, then.
I can't, my power cable doesn't stretch that far.

What do you get if you cross a computer with an elephant?
Lots of memory.

Mother robot: Stop being so antisocial and come down and meet our guests.
Son robot: I'm not antisocial – I'm just not user-friendly.

What kind of car does a robot drive?
A volts-wagon.

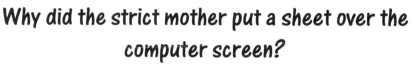

Why did the strict mother put a sheet over the computer screen?
Because she didn't want her kids to pick up bad language from the cursor.

How do turtles stay in touch?
They use shell-ular phones.

Why did the computer throw its lunch in the garbage?
It looked like spam.

Why did the car blush?
It saw the traffic light changing.

What was the inscription on the robot grave?
"Rust in Pieces"

RUST
IN
PIECES

Why did the inventor stuff herbs in the disk drive of his computer?
He was trying to build a thyme machine.

How do you fix a robotic gorilla?
With a monkey wrench.

What was wrong with the robot shepherd?
He didn't have enough RAM.

How many ears does a robot have?
Three: a left ear, a right ear, and just in case they go wrong, an engine-ear.

What do you call a man with a car on his head?
Jack!

Why couldn't the computer take its hat off?
Because the caps lock was on.

Spotted in the library:
How to Fix Just About Anything by Andy Mann.

What do you call a short band leader?
A semi-conductor.

Teacher: Look at the state of the classroom computer. I want that screen cleaned so well I can see my own face in it!
Pupil: But then it will crack!

Why shouldn't you trust someone who always types in upper case?
There is something very shifty about them.

Did you hear about the coffee-drinking robot?
Boy, was he ever wired!

Why did the steel robot have so many friends?
He had a magnetic personality.

Can you spell "user-friendly computer" in just four letters?
E, Z, P, C!

Where do cars go swimming?
In a carpool.

Why did the robot swimmer need so many lessons?
Because he kept getting rusty.

Why did the computer catch a cold?
Someone kept leaving its Windows open.

Why did the PC keep sneezing?
It had a computer virus.

What was wrong with the environmentally friendly flashlight?
It relied on solar power.

Did you hear about the cyborg's expensive new limbs?
They cost him an arm and a leg!

Why do robots make great stuntmen?
Because they have nerves of steel.

Why did they have to call off the computer race?
The competitors kept crashing.

How do trees get on the Internet?
They log in.

What do you call a robot standing in the rain?
Rusty!

What invention is sillier than glow-in-the-dark sunglasses for midnight sunbathing?
Underwater umbrellas for scuba divers!

Why did the silly girl put her letters in the microwave?
She wanted to use Hotmail.

Who won the Oscar for best
android actor?
Robot Downey, Jr.

How did the scientist invent
insect repellent?
He started from scratch.

Why didn't the computer
mouse cross the road?
It's lead wasn't long enough.

What happened when the
bossy android charged
for too long?
It went on a power trip!

Why did the computer programmer give up his life
of crime?
He couldn't hack it any more.

Do you think scientists will ever invent flying desserts?
No, that's pie in the sky.

Have you been on the optician's website?
It's a site for sore eyes.

How did the lazy office worker get his daily exercise?
He clicked on "run" on his computer.

Why didn't two computers get along?
They got their wires crossed.

How do lazy spiders decorate their homes?
They hire web designers.

What do you call a nervous robot?
A shy-borg.

Teacher: Why have you stopped typing?

Pupil: It was making me feel keyed up.

Did you hear about the computer programmer whose illegal activities made him sick?

He gave himself a hacking cough.

Did you have any success with Internet dating?

Yes, it was love at first site.

What do you call an android with oars?

A row-bot.

How do you catch a computer thief?
With a mousetrap.

How did the computer
get out of prison?
It used its
"escape" key.

What Internet site do
sheep like to visit?
Ewe tube.

Why did the little robot start to cry?
He was missing his motherboard.

Do you think teleportation will ever be possible?
That's neither here nor there.

Which way did the outlaw go after he stole
the computer?
He went data way.

Did you hear
about the
unhappy android?
It had a chip on
its shoulder!

Why did the computer
programmer call
pest control?
His software was
full of bugs!

What sort of net do you
use to catch robot fish?
A mag-net.

Teacher: Can you think of a password with
eight characters?
Pupil: How about "Snow White
and the Seven Dwarves?"

What do you call a robot pig?
A sty-borg.

Why did the girl mouse decide not to ask the boy mouse out on a second date?

They just didn't click.

Computer repair man: What's wrong with this laptop, sir?

Customer: Thespacebarseemstobestuck.

Have you heard about the new online service for shortsighted people?

It's called the Squinternet.

What did one calculator say to the other calculator?

You can count on me.

Why did the computer go crazy?
It had a screw loose.

How do you stop batteries from running out?
Hide their shoes.

How does a tiny robot say goodbye?
With a micro-wave.

What do you call a robot that always takes the longest route?
R2 Detour.

Did you hear about the little robot who looked
just like his dad?
He was a microchip off the old block.

MONSTER FUN

Where do ghosts swim?
In the Dead Sea.

What did the vampire doctor say?
Necks please!

Did you hear about the banshee who wanted to be an actress?
She did a scream test.

What does a dragon
call a knight in helmet
and breastplate?
Tinned food!

What do you get if you cross a
vampire and a circus entertainer?
Someone who goes straight for
the juggler!

What do ghosts eat for dinner?
Goulash!

How do ghosts begin business
letters?
"Tomb it may concern..."

What do you get if you cross
a vampire with a mummy?
Something you wouldn't want
to unwrap!

Why didn't the skeleton fight the monster?
He didn't have the guts!

What has a pointy hat, a broomstick, and a blue face?
A witch holding her breath.

How can you tell when there's a giant monster under your bed?
When your nose touches the ceiling.

What happened to the vampire with bad breath?
His dentist told him to gargoyle twice a day!

What do vampires do at eleven o'clock every night?
They have a coffin break.

Why did Miss Skeleton go to the beautician?
For a bone-icure!

How do you know that smoking is harmful to
your health?
Well, look what happened to all the dragons!

Should monsters eat people on an empty stomach?
No, they should eat them on a plate!

What do you get if you cross Bambi with a ghost?
Bamboo!

Why don't skeletons sing
church music?
They have no organs.

What goes "WOO-HA-HA"
THUMP?
Frankenstein's monster
laughing his head off.

What job does Dracula have with the Transylvanian baseball team?

He looks after the bats!

Why do ghosts never feel guilty?

They have a clear conscience!

First friend: Did you know that you can get fur from a vampire?

Second friend: Really? What kind of fur?

First friend: As fur away as possible!

Why did the car stop when it saw the monster truck?

It had a nervous breakdown.

Why was young
Dr Frankenstein
so popular?
Because he was
great at making
new friends!

How did you know
I was a ghost?
Oh, I can see right
through you!

How did the ghostly teacher make sure his pupils had
learned what he had written on the board?
He went through it again!

Why did the monster buy an axe?
Because he wanted to get a-head in life!

How do vampires get clean?
In a blood bath!

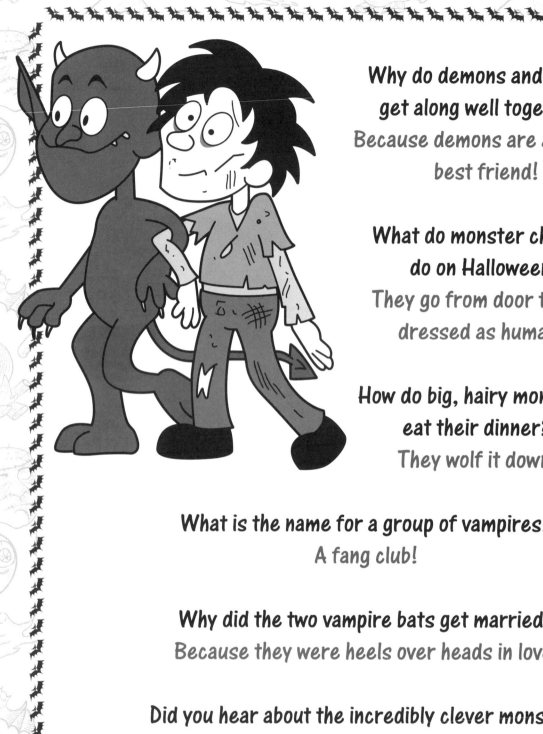

Why do demons and ghouls
get along well together?
Because demons are a ghoul's
best friend!

What do monster children
do on Halloween?
They go from door to door
dressed as humans!

How do big, hairy monsters
eat their dinner?
They wolf it down!

What is the name for a group of vampires?
A fang club!

Why did the two vampire bats get married?
Because they were heels over heads in love!

Did you hear about the incredibly clever monster?
He was called Frank Einstein.

Why do ghosts go back to the same place every year
for their holiday?
They like their old haunts best!

Why didn't the skeleton go to the ball?
It had no body to go with.

What do the police call it
when they watch a
vampire's house?
A stake out!

Where did Dracula
open his bank account?
At a blood bank!

What will a vampire
never order in
a restaurant?
Steak.

What sort of telescope lets you see ghosts?
A horrorscope!

Where do werewolves live?
In warehouses.

Who do vampires invite to their birthday parties?
Anybody they can dig up!

Why did Dracula advertise for a housekeeper?
He wanted some new blood in the house!

Who is the world's scariest superhero?
Vampire bat-man!

Why doesn't Dracula have any friends?
Because he's a pain in the neck!

Why wasn't the werewolf astronaut allowed to land his spaceship?
Because the Moon was full!

What did Dr Frankenstein do when the monster's head kept falling off?
He made a bolt for it!

Why do monsters like to stand in a ring?
They love being part of a vicious circle!

What does Dracula drink?
De-coffin-ated coffee!

What do you call a lazy skeleton?
Bone idle!

How does Frankenstein's monster sit in a chair?
Bolt upright!

What did the old vampire say when he broke his teeth?
Fangs for the memory...

What does it say on the mummy's garage entrance?
Toot, and come in!

"Hurry up," said the father skeleton to his son,
"or you'll be late for the skull bus!"

Why did Godzilla stop eating
buildings?
He got atomic ache!

Who was the winner of the
headless horseman race?
No one. They all finished
neck and neck!

Why did the giant robot feel
sick after eating a train?
He caught a commuter
virus!

Why are you throwing garlic out of the window?
To keep vampires away.
But there aren't any vampires here.
See – it works!

If having hairy palms is the first sign of turning into
a monster, what is the second?
Looking for them!

Why did the monster have twins in his lunchbox?
In case he felt like seconds!

What do monsters call a crowded swimming pool?
Soup!

Why did the werewolf swallow a bag full of coins?
Because he thought the change would do him good!

Why do zombies always look so tired?
They are dead on their feet!

What is the first thing
a monster eats
when he goes to a
restaurant?
The waiter!

Why didn't the
vampire laugh at the
joke about the
wooden stake?
He didn't get the point!

Why did the robot need
a manicure?
He had rusty nails!

Why didn't the phantom win the lottery?
He didn't have a ghost of a chance!

Why do soccer teams have to work so hard
when they play against zombies?
Because they face stiff competition!

What did the young ghost call his mother and father?
His trans-parents!

Why do little monsters not mind being eaten by ghosts?
Because they know they will always be in good spirits!

Why are there more ghost cats than ghost dogs?
Because every cat has nine lives!

Why do monster parents tell their children to eat their cabbage?
Because they want them to have a healthy green complexion!

Why did the cyclops school close down?
Because they only had one pupil!

Why are vampires stupid?
Because blood is thicker than water!

Why do other monsters find mummies vain?
They're so wrapped up in themselves.

Why do vampires never invite trolls to their dinner parties?
They can't stand all that goblin!

What do you call a ghostly chicken?

A poultry-geist.

Why did the zombie go to the pharmacy?

He wanted something to help stop his coffin.

What do you call a child vampire?

A pain in the knee!

Who do vampires invite to their weddings?

All their blood relatives!

How does a skeleton know when it's going to rain?
He just gets a feeling in his bones!

Why don't ghosts do aerobics?
Because they don't want to be exorcised!

Why are owls so brave at night?
Because they don't give a hoot for ghosts, monsters, or vampires!

How do vampires show affection for each other?
They bat their eyelids!

What is the first thing you should put into a haunted house?
Someone else!

Why did Goldilocks go to Egypt?
She wanted to see the mummy bear!

What did the werewolf say to the skeleton?
It's been so nice getting to gnaw you!

Why did the ghost go to the bicycle shop?
He needed some new spooks for his front wheel!

What do you get if you cross the Abominable Snowman and Count Dracula?
Severe frostbite!

What do you need to pick up a giant's cutlery?
A forklift.

Knock knock!
Who's there?
Russia!
Russia who?
Russia way – a monster's coming!

What did the witch call her baby daughter?
Wanda!

What do you call a male
vampire in women's
clothing?
Drag-cula!

Why was the genie of
the lamp angry?
Someone rubbed him up
the wrong way!

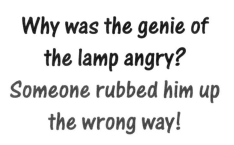

What do you get if you cross a warlock and a laptop?
A computer wizard!

What do skeletons say before eating?
Bone appetit!

What do you call the jewels that ghosts wear?
Tombstones!

What do dinosaurs rest their teacups on?
Tyrannosaucers.

How do you help Frankenstein's monster?
Give him a hand when he needs it!

How do witch children listen to stories?
Spellbound!

What kinds of
roads are haunted
by ghosts?
Dead ends!

What do you
call a hairy
monster that's lost
its way home?
A where-am-I wolf.

What drink do monsters slurp?
Lemon and slime.

Book spotted at the school library:
The Haunted House by Hugo First.

What happens when a witch catches the flu?
Everyone gets a cold spell!

Why do vampires have a steady nerve?
They are as ghoul as cucumbers!

Why don't vampires write their own books?
They prefer to use ghost writers!

Where do monsters like to go on vacation?
Death Valley!

Why do sea monsters go to so many parties?
Because they always have a whale of a time!

What do you call monster children?
Ghouls and boils.

Dad, what is a werewolf?
Be quiet and comb your face!

What do Abominable Snowmen sing at parties?
"Freeze a jolly good fellow..."

Why are monsters forgetful?
Because everything goes in one ear and out the others.

What do baby sea monsters play with?
Doll-fins!

What happened when the yeti ate a curry?
He blew his cool.

Which monster is the
most untidy?
The Loch Mess Monster!

What animals do vampires
like best?
Giraffes.

What do mummies
do to relax?
They just unwind a little!

Why can you never get
through to a vampire bat
on the phone?
Because they always
hang up!

What kind of mistakes do young ghosts make at school?
Boo-boo s.

Why did King Kong rush up the Empire State Building
in New York?
He had a plane to catch.

What was the name of the ghost who ate too much porridge?
Ghoul-dilocks.

Why are so few ghosts ever arrested?
Because it's so hard to pin anything on them.

What do you call a little monster with a wooden leg?
A hoblin-goblin.

Why are vampires such good comedians?
Because of their biting wit.

What happened to the naughtiest witch in the class?
She was ex-spelled!

Which monster has the best hearing?
That depends on which one is the eeriest.

How did the mother monster stop her son from biting his nails?
She cut his fingers off.

What do you call a kind, helpful monster who likes flowers and butterflies?
A failure!

Why don't witches wear sombreros?
Because there's no point.

What pets does Dracula own?
A bloodhound and a ghoul-fish!

**What happened to the
ghostly comedian?**
He was booed off the stage.

**What happened to the ghost
who got lost in the fog?**
He is now sadly mist.

Why do skeletons hate winter?
Because the cold goes right
through them!

**Why did King Kong join
the army?**
To learn about gorilla
warfare.

Where do you find
monster snails?
On the end of
monsters' fingers!

Why do vampires dislike
computers?
They hate anything
new-fang-led!

What do ghosts do if they are afraid?
Hide under a sheet!

How do you make a skeleton laugh?
Just tickle his funny bone.

Why are vampires good at treating people
with coughs?
Because they can clear your throat in seconds!

JOLLY JUNGLE

Why should you never trust a giraffe?
They are always telling tall stories.

What flies through the jungle singing opera?
The Parrots of Penzance.

Teacher: What do you think a pair of alligator
shoes would cost?
Pupil: That would depend on the size of
your alligator's feet!

Is it a good idea to buy
a pet skunk?
Yes, it makes a lot of
scents!

Why do elephants
paint their
toenails red?
So they can
hide in cherry
trees!

Why do elephants never forget?
Because no one ever tells them anything.

Why was the cobra thrown out of the snake club?
Because he wasn't a mamba.

**What should you do if you find a tiger asleep
on your bed?**
Sleep on the couch!

Why are anteaters never ill?
Because they're full of anty-bodies.

What do wasps do when they build a new nest?
They have a house-swarming party.

What do you get if
you cross a parrot
with a centipede?
A walkie talkie.

Why were the
sweet potatoes playing
jazz music?
They were having
a yam session.

What do you call a lion
with no eyes?
Lon!

Why should you never surprise a parrot perching
on a doorknob?
Because it might fly off the handle!

What happened when the skunk fell in the river?
It stank all the way to the bottom.

How can you tell the difference between an African elephant and an Indian elephant?
Look at their passports!

What do elephants take to help them sleep?
Trunkquilizers!

Why can't I get the king of the jungle on the telephone?
Because the lion is busy!

Who won the giraffe race?
Nobody knows – the competitors were neck and neck!

What's brown, weighs as much as a truck, and bounces?
A bungee-jumping elephant.

What do you give a snake with a headache?
Asp-irin.

Teacher: Have you written your essay on big cats?
Pupil: I thought it would be safer to use paper!

What do you call a lion with toothache?
Rory!

What do you call a hippo that always claims to be sick?
A hippochondriac.

Why did the firefly keep crashing?
He wasn't very bright.

What did King Kong say when he was told that his sister had had a baby?
Well, I'll be a monkey's uncle!

What sort of dancing will elephants do in your front room?
Break dancing!

Why do birds of paradise have such amazing plumage?
They pay attention to de-tail.

Why don't fruit bats live alone?
They like to hang out with their friends.

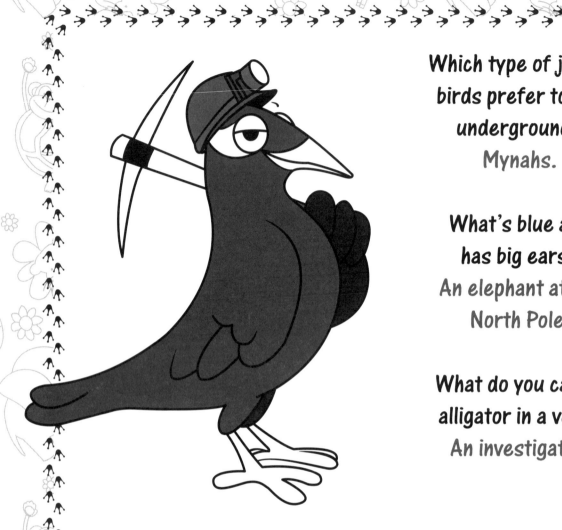

Which type of jungle
birds prefer to live
underground?
Mynahs.

What's blue and
has big ears?
An elephant at the
North Pole.

What do you call an
alligator in a vest?
An investigator.

How does a lion like his steak?
Medium roar.

How do you get into the jungle monastery?
With a monk-key.

What do you call a show full of lions?
The mane event.

What do you call a fashionable big cat?
A dandy lion.

What do you get if you cross a gorilla with a porcupine?
A seat on the bus!

How do you fix a
broken chimp?
With a monkey
wrench!

What do you get
if you cross a tiger
and a sheep?
A striped sweater.

What do you get
if you cross a snake
with a kangaroo?
A jump rope.

How does a lion greet other creatures?
"Very pleased to eat you!"

Why did King Kong climb up the side of the
Empire State Building?
The elevator was broken.

What game do cannibals like playing?
Swallow the leader.

Baby snake: Dad, are we
poisonous?
Dad snake: No, son, why
do you ask?
Baby snake: I've just bitten
my tongue!

What do you call an alligator
private eye?
An investi-gator.

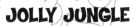

What do you get if you cross a tarantula with a rose?
We're not sure, but don't try smelling it!

Why don't bananas sunbathe?
Because they would peel.

What happens if you cross a hummingbird with a doorbell?
You get a humdinger.

What does the lemur do every evening?
He curls up with a nice long tail.

Why does a frog
have more lives
than a cat?
Because it croaks
every night.

What do ape lawyers
study in college?
The law of the jungle.

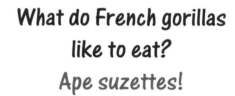

What do French gorillas
like to eat?
Ape suzettes!

Is it hard to spot a leopard?
Not at all – they come that way!

What advice did the parrot give to the toucan?
Talk is cheep.

What do toucans sing at Christmas?
Jungle Bells.

Why was the salamander lost?

He was newt to the area.

How did the monkey get down the stairs?

It slid down the banana-ster.

What did the snake give his date when he dropped her off?

He gave her a good-night hiss.

Why did the leopard refuse to take a bath?

Because he didn't want to become spotless.

What happened at the cannibals' wedding?
They toasted the bride and groom.

Why should you never tell a giraffe a secret?
Because you could fall off his neck as you whisper
in his ear.

What did Tarzan tell his son?
"Be careful – it's a jungle out there."

What's sweet and
crunchy and swings
through the trees?
A meringue-utan.

What's worse than
a crocodile with a
toothache?
A centipede with
athlete's foot.

What kind of
ice cream do gorillas
like best?
Chocolate chimp.

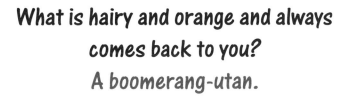

Why do giraffes
have small appetites?
Because a little goes
a long way.

What happens if you
upset a cannibal?
You get into hot water.

What is hairy and orange and always
comes back to you?
A boomerang-utan.

What is brown, has huge wings, and gives
money to elephants?
The tusk fairy.

Which animals were the last to leave Noah's Ark?
The elephants – they had to pack their trunks.

What did the banana say to the gorilla?
Nothing, bananas can't talk!

What happens if you cross an elephant and a canary?
You get a very messy cage.

Why do birds fly south for the winter?
Because it's too far to walk.

What's the most dangerous animal in your backyard?
The clothes-lion.

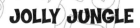

What do you call an exploding ape?
A ba-BOOM!

What do you get if you cross a snake with a pig?
A boar constrictor.

What do snakes have written on their bath towels?
Hiss and hers!

What do you get
if you cross a gorilla
with a prisoner?
A kong-vict!

Why did the leopard
eat the tightrope
walker?
He wanted to have
a balanced diet.

What did the python do when it saw the lion?
It recoiled!

What's the best time to buy parakeets?
When they're going cheep.

How do you make an elephant fly?
Start with a very long zipper.

Why does Tarzan shout so loudly?
Because it hurts when he pounds his chest.

What do you call two rhinos on a bicycle?
Optimistic.

Teacher: They say time flies
like an arrow.
Pupil: Yes, but fruit flies like a banana.

What would you get if a python slipped into a tuba?
A snake in the brass.

What has 99 legs and one eye?
A pirate centipede.

What has three trunks, two tails, and six feet?
An elephant with spare parts.

Why couldn't the butterfly go to the dance?
Because it was a moth ball.

How do snails fight in the jungle?
They slug it out!

What do you give a gorilla that's going to throw up?
Plenty of room!

What did the queen bee say to her nosy
friend next door?
Mind your own bees' nest.

What's the most popular lesson at snake school?
Hisssstory.

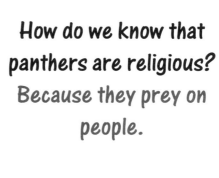

How do we know that
panthers are religious?
Because they prey on
people.

What sort of animal
is big, likes mud, and wears
flowers in its hair?
A hippy-potamus.

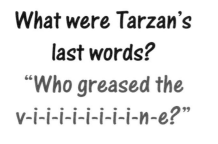

What were Tarzan's last words?
"Who greased the v-i-i-i-i-i-i-i-n-e?"

Knock, knock!
Who's there?
Giraffe.
Giraffe who?
Giraffe to ask me that stupid question?

How do you make orange crush?
Get an elephant to jump up and down in the fruit and vegetable aisle!

How do hippos commute?
By hippopotabus.

What looks like half an anteater?
The other half.

How did the rival apes settle their differences?
With a gorilla war.

What do you get if you cross an elephant with a parrot?
An animal that tells you everything it remembers.

How do fleas travel about the jungle?
They itch-hike.

Why did the canary refuse to work in a coal mine?
He said it was beneath him.

What did the tiger say when he cut off his tail?
It won't be long now.

What do you call a rabbit that can beat up a lion?
Sir.

Why should you value an elephant's opinion?
Because it carries a lot of weight.

What do you call a snail on a turtle's shell?
A thrill seeker.

What do chimps learn at school?
The ape-B-C's.

What line of work did the parrot take up after it swallowed a clock?
Politics.

What's the medical term for memory loss in parrots?
Polynesia.

Why did the monkey take the banana to see the doctor?
Because it wasn't peeling well.

How do you start a firefly race?
By saying "On your marks, get set, glow!"

Why did the hippo eat a couch and three chairs?
Because he had a suite tooth.

What happened when the tree frog parked in a no-parking space?
It got toad away!

Why did Tarzan spend so much time on the golf course?
He was perfecting his swing.

Which jungle animals are terrified
of vampires?
Giraffes – they have such long necks!

Where do monkeys go if they lose their tails?
To the retail store.

Why does a flamingo lift up one leg?
Because if it lifted up both legs it would fall over!

What did the ape call his first wife?
His prime mate.

How much does a lion trainer need to know?
More than the lion!

Where do monkeys pick up juicy gossip?
On the apevine.

How did the cannibal commit suicide?
He got himself into a real stew.

If a dictionary goes from A to Z, what goes from Z to A?
A zebra.

How do gorillas stay in shape?
They join jungle gyms.

What do you call a
failed lion tamer?
Claude Bottom!

Why don't farmers grow
bananas any longer?
Because they're long enough
already.

How does the veterinarian dentist check the
tiger for cavities?
Very carefully!

Why was the panther sick after he'd eaten a priest?
It's hard to keep a good man down.

First man: I took my son to the zoo last week.
Second man: Really? And which cage is he in now?

What is the difference between a wet day
and an injured tiger?

One pours with rain and the other roars with pain.

Knock, knock!

Who's there?

Toucan.

Toucan who?

Toucan play at that game.

Did you hear about the
snake archer?

He used a boa
and arrow.

Did you hear about
the crocodile
who took up
photography?

He was snap-happy.

OUTER SPACE

Where do you find black holes?
In black socks.

What makes you think my son could be an astronaut?
He has nothing but space between his ears!

What do you call a wizard from outer space?
A flying sorcerer.

Which weighs the most, a full Moon or a half Moon?
A half Moon, because a full Moon is much lighter!

What happens to
astronauts who
misbehave?
They're grounded.

How do you get a
baby astronaut to
go to sleep?
Rocket.

Knock knock.
Who's there?
Jupiter.
Jupiter who?
Jupiter spaceship
on my lawn?

Which is the most
glamorous planet?
Saturn. It has a
lot of rings.

Teacher: William, how fast does light travel?
William: I don't know – it's already arrived by
the time I wake up!

When can you be sure that the Moon won't eat you?
When it's a full Moon.

What crazy bug lives on the Moon?
The lunar tick.

How do aliens go fishing?
With Earthworms!

Why do little green men have nice, warm homes?
Because they live in little greenhouses!

An astronaut and a chimp were fired off into space.
The chimp opened its sealed orders, read them,
and immediately started programming the flight computer.
The astronaut opened his sealed orders and
found only one instruction:
"Feed the chimp!"

Three badly made robots were playing cards.

The first one threw his hand in.

The second one rolled his eyes.

The third one laughed his head off.

What do you call a loony spaceman?

An astronut.

Book spotted in the school library:

Is There Life on Mars? by Howard I. No.

Why didn't the astronaut get burned when he
landed on the Sun?
He went there at night!

Some meteorites collide with planets.
What do you call meteorites that miss?
Meteowrongs.

What do robot office workers eat?
A staple diet.

Asteroid 1: Hi. Looks like we're in for a shower.
Asteroid 2: Yes. Pleased to meteor!

What do aliens cook their breakfasts on?
Unidentified frying objects.

What do young astronauts sit on during takeoff?
Booster seats.

How does the Solar System hold up its trousers?
With an asteroid belt.

What did the boy star say to the girl star?
Do you want to glow out with me?

Why did the alien build a spaceship from feathers?
He wanted to travel light years!

What did one rocket say to the other?
I wish I could quit smoking!

What do aliens toast over the fire?
Martian-mallows.

Why do astronauts have to prepare a meal before blastoff?
They get hungry at launch time.

What holds the Moon up?
Moon beams.

Why was the thirsty astronaut hanging around near the computer keyboard?
He was looking for the space bar.

Big alien: If this planet is Mars, what's that one over there?
Little alien: Is it Pa's?

Did you hear about the alien who sat up all night wondering where the Sun had gone?
The next morning it dawned on him!

Why don't astronauts keep their jobs for long?
Because after their training they're always fired.

Did you know that they have found life on another planet?
Really?
Yes, there are fleas on Pluto!

Why is an alien such a good gardener?
Because he has green fingers.

Why are grandma's teeth like stars?
Because they come out at night.

Where do you leave your spaceship when you visit another planet?
At a parking meteor!

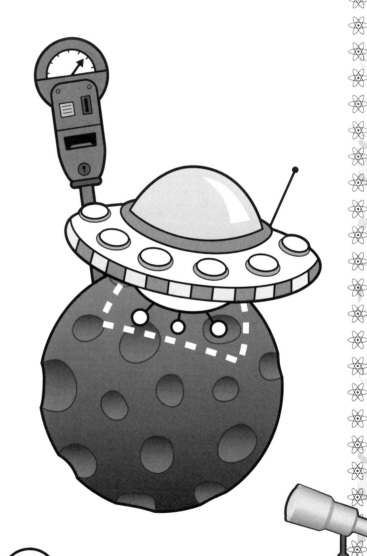

What's an astronomer?
A night watchman with a college education.

Which actor won the Martian Oscars?
Kevin Outer-Spacey!

Why do astronauts never diet?
No one needs to lose weight in space, because
everything is weightless!

**Why did the spaceship land outside
my bedroom?**
You must have left the landing light on!

**What do aliens like
to drink?**
Gravi-tea.

**What did Saturn say
when Jupiter asked if he
could call him?**
"Don't call me – I'll give
you a ring."

What's normal eyesight for a Martian?
20-20-20!

Why wouldn't you want Saturn to take a bath?
Because he'd leave a ring around the tub.

How do you organize a party in space?
You planet!

**I don't know what to buy my friend the space alien for
his birthday.**
How about five and a half pairs of slippers?

What does an alien gardener do with his hedges?
Eclipse them every spring!

Why did the alien launch a clock into space?
He wanted to see time fly.

How did the alien tie his shoelaces?
With an astro-knot.

Why don't aliens celebrate each other's birthdays?
They don't like to give away their presents.

What did the big star say to the little star?

You're too young to go out at night!

What kind of star wears sunglasses?

A movie star.

When is a window like a star?

When it's a skylight.

If an athlete gets athlete's foot, what does an astronaut get?

Missile toe!

What is covered in wool and comes from outer space?

A ewe-F-O.

Why couldn't the alien's spaceship travel at the speed of light?
Because he took off in the dark!

How did the aliens hurt the farmer?
They landed on his corn.

When is the Moon not hungry?
When it is full.

What do you call an overweight alien?
An extra-cholesterol.

How many Martians does it take to screw in a light bulb?
Millions! One to hold the bulb, and the rest to turn the planet.

What music do astronauts play?
Rocket and roll.

Which is more useful, the Sun or the Moon?
The Moon – because it shines at night when you want the light. The Sun shines during the day, when you don't really need it!

Spotted on the science shelf of the school library:
Fly Me to the Moon
by Tay Cough.

How does an astronaut say he is sorry?
He apollo-gises.

Why are astronauts such successful people?
They always go up in the world.

What do you call a sick space monster?
An ailin' alien.

I've given up on time travel.
Why?
There's no future in it.

Living on Earth may be expensive – but it does include
a free trip around the Sun each year.

Why are there no Martian tourists at the Grand Canyon?
Because it looks so much like home!

What did the alien say to the service pump?
"Don't you know that it's rude to stick your finger in your ear
when I'm talking to you?"

How do aliens stay clean?
They take meteor showers.

How do you phone the Sun?
You use a Sun-dial.

**Mars got sent to prison
after the big robbery trial.
Why? He wasn't even there!
Yes, but he helped
to planet.**

What is a light year?
The same as a normal year,
but with fewer calories.

What did the astronaut say to his alien girlfriend?
"You're out of this world!"

How do computers make jumpers?
On the interknit.

Why does Superman wear such big shoes?
Because of his amazing feats.

What board game do aliens like to play?
Moon-opoly!

Why do astronauts find it hard to mix with other people?
They're not really down to Earth.

How do astronauts serve drinks?
In sunglasses.

How do aliens keep from falling over in a spaceship?
They Klingon.

Why do cats hate flying saucers?
Because they can't reach the milk!

First astronomer: Do you think there's intelligent
life out there?

Second astronomer: I doubt it. All the aliens
I've met are pretty stupid!

Did you hear about the resentful robot?

He had a microchip on his shoulder.

What should you do if you meet a little green man?

Come back when he's a little riper.

Clones are people, two.

How do Martians count
to fifteen?
On their fingers.

Which river-dwelling
animals are really
aliens?
Otters – they come
from otter space!

If astronauts are so
smart, why do they always
count backward?

Have you seen the film about toads in space?
It's called Star Warts.

What did the loser in the astronomy contest receive?
The constellation prize.

How do Martians shave?
With laser blades.

Which relative visits astronauts in outer space?
Auntie Gravity.

Pupil: When is the lecture on time travel?
Teacher: It will be held two weeks ago.

First ground controller: Man, that astronaut is totally crazy.
Second ground controller: Yes, he's a real space cadet!

Which are the dreamiest scientists?
Astronomers, because they have stars in their eyes.

What happened to the astronaut who stepped on chewing gum?
He got stuck in orbit.

What's made from potatoes and is
10,000 light years away?
A space chip!

Why did the steel robot have so many friends?
It must have been his magnetic personality!

What poems do astronauts read?
Uni-verse!

What did the alien say
to the cat?
Take me to your litter.

What goes MOOZ?
A spaceship reversing.

Why did the alien family have to move house?
Because they were all spaced out.

Knock knock!
Who's there?
Athena.
Athena who?
Athena shooting star last night.

Which planet is
shaped like a fish?
Nep-tuna.

What do you call a
really noisy spaceship?
A space racket.

Shy traffic light to the alien:
"Don't look at me while
I'm changing."

Knock knock!
Who's there?
Detail.
Detail who?
De-tail is de-end of de-comet.

What did the astronaut wear on his day off?
Apollo shirt.

What do giant aliens do with astronauts?
They put them in the cupboard, with all the other tinned food!

What lightweight tool can you use to fix a spaceship?
A pocket rocket sprocket!

How is an alien crop circle like a lame joke?
Because they're both corny.

What did the greedy alien say?
"Take me to your larder!"

What do meteors like to read?
Comet books!

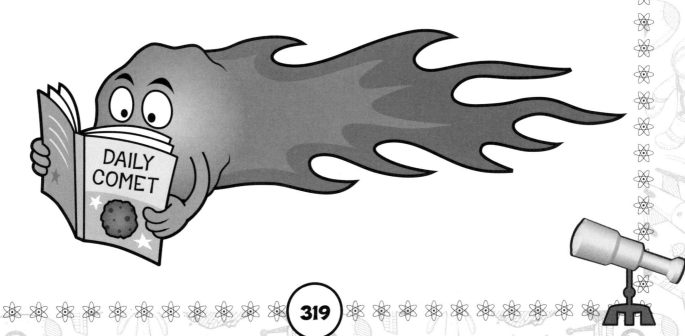

How many planets are out in space?

All of them.

What injections do sick rockets get?

Booster shots.

What did the Martian painter say to the Earth painter?

Take me to your ladder.

What did the romantic Moon monster say to his girlfriend?
"Let's go for a walk. There's a beautiful Earth out tonight!"

What do you call a dog who lives on the Moon?
Moon Rover.

Why is space exploration such good value?
Because people's tax money goes farther than ever before.

What kind of extraterrestrial villain works in a restaurant?
Darth Waiter.

Why was the spaceship bent?
It had been going at warp speed.

How do you find
a cow in space?
Follow the Milky Way.

How many ears does
Captain Kirk have?
Three – a right ear,
a left ear, and a final
frontier!

First Martian, just landed in Rome:
Which do you think is further away,
London or the Moon?
Second Martian: Don't be silly – can you see
London from here?

Why don't astronauts relate well to other people?
They are not always down-to-earth.

Why was Pluto squashed flat?
Because Mars Saturn Pluto!

How is medicine packaged for astronauts?
In space capsules.

Pupil: I want to be an astronaut when I grow up.
Teacher: Well, you certainly have high hopes!

How do you say farewell to a two-headed alien?
"Bye bye bye bye!"

**What do astronauts
eat out of?**
Satellite dishes.

**How did the inventor
of the space rocket feel?**
Over the moon!

**How did the inventor of the
jetpack feel?**
He was on cloud nine!

Spotted in the library:
The Easy Way to Fly by Otto Pilot.

**Why did the alien turn the restaurant staff
upside down?**
Someone told him that you had to tip the waiter!

Why do astronomers always bang their heads?
It helps them to see stars!

MAGICAL MAYHEM

What happens when
a witch on a broomstick
brakes too hard?
She flies off the handle.

How do witches tell the time?
With witch watches.

Where does the wizards' school store its
weightlifting equipment?
Behind the dumbbell door.

How do elves greet each other?
"Small world, isn't it?"

How do Jamaican ghosts style their hair?
In deadlocks!

What happened to the witch who swallowed a poisonous toad?
She croaked!

What do you call a witch's garage?
A broom closet.

Who scared the troll under the bridge?
The billy ghosts Gruff.

Which jokes go down well with skeletons?
Rib ticklers!

Who said, "Get lost" to the Big Bad Wolf?
Little Rude Riding Hood.

What do you call
a fairy that has never
taken a bath?
Stinkerbell!

What do you
get if you cross
a skeleton and
a dog?
An animal that
buries itself!

What has six legs and flies through the air?
A witch and her cat on a broomstick.

What did the headless ghost get when he fell
through a window?
A pane in the neck!

What do witches sing at Christmas?
Deck the Halls with Poison Ivy.

What is a wizzerd?
A wizard who can't spell!

Why is Frankenstein's monster bad at school?
He doesn't have the brains he was born with!

How many guests has the zombie invited to his party?
It depends on who he could dig up!

Why did the pixie move out of the toadstool?
Because there wasn't mushroom.

What's big, red, and eats rocks?
A big, red rock-eater!

What do ghostly policemen do?
They haunt down criminals!

Why don't giants speak to leprechauns?
They're no good at small talk.

How do you make an ogre's
eyes light up?
Shine a flashlight in his ear.

What do you call
two witches who
live together?
Broommates!

Why would Snow White be a good judge?
Because she was the fairest in the land.

What do Italian ghosts eat for dinner?
Spookhetti!

Why are black cats good singers?
They are very mewsical.

Why was the skeleton's jacket in shreds?
Because he had very sharp shoulder blades!

Where do you normally find elves?
It depends where you left them!

Which fairy-tale creature has the most teeth?
A dragon?
No, the tooth fairy!

Baby ogre: When I grow up, I want to drive a tank!
Mother ogre: Well, I certainly won't stand in your way!

What did the No Parking sign outside the witch's house say?
"Violators will be toads!"

How do two ghosts decide who owns something?
They fright each other for it!

What goes cackle, squelch, cackle, squelch?
A witch in soggy shoes.

What noise does a witch's car make?
Broom, broom!

What do you call a vampire that hides in the kitchen?
Spatula!

Why did the headless
ghost go to the
psychiatrist?
Because he wasn't
all there!

What do you call a
magician's assistant?
Magic Trixie!

What type of spells did the
whirling wizard cast?
Dizzy spells.

Why didn't the witch sing a solo at the concert?
Because she had a frog in her throat.

Why was the ogre catching centipedes?
He wanted scrambled legs for breakfast!

Where would you find a suitable gift for
a tortured ghost?
In a chain store!

What did the police
do to the giant who ran
away with the circus?
They made him bring it
back.

Which great detective
is three feet tall and
has pointed ears?
Sherlock Gnomes.

What is the difference
between a dragon
and a mouse?
Have you had your eyes
tested recently?

Did you hear about the
vampire who fell asleep in
the wrong coffin?
It was a grave mistake!

Knock, knock.
Who's there?
Aladdin.
Aladdin who?
Aladdin the street who wants to come in!

What happened to the boxer who got knocked out
by Dracula?
He was out for the Count.

Why can't you borrow
money from a leprechaun?
Because he's always
a little short.

How do you keep an idiot
in suspense?
I'll tell you tomorrow!

What did the monster say
to the scruffy werewolf?
"You look like you're going
to the dogs!"

What did the big candle say to the little candle?
I'm going out tonight.

Did you hear about the tiny, winged Egyptian king?
He was a fairy pharaoh!

How do you fix a jack-o'-lantern?
Use a pumpkin patch.

How do you make a witch itch?
Take away the W!

I'm never going to follow in my father's footsteps;
I faint at the sight of blood!
Was your father a doctor?
No, a vampire!

What do you call a nervous witch?
A twitch.

Who do wizards stop for on the highway?
Witch-hikers.

Who is the scariest player on a soccer team?
The ghoulie.

Did you hear about the failed magician?
He had one half brother and one half sister!

Why do witches have painful joints?
They get broomatism.

Who lights up a haunted house?
The lights witch.

Did you hear about
the enchanted bike
that went around
biting people?
It was a vicious cycle!

What happened to the little girl who slept with her head under the pillow?
The tooth fairy took all her teeth away!

What fruit do vegetarian vampires eat?
Blood oranges.

What's brown and hairy and flies through the air, cackling?
A witch in a gorilla suit.

Little brother: There's an ogre at the door with a really ugly face.
Big brother: Tell him you already have one!

Did you hear about the girl who put her granny's false teeth under her pillow?
The tooth fairy left her a fake bank note!

Why are witches
convinced they're funny?
Because every time
they look in the mirror
it cracks up.

What does the
Abominable Snowman
like to eat?
Spag-yeti.

What do you call a girl with a
frog on her head?
Lily!

What did the doctor say to the invisible man after he had
swallowed some coins?
"I can see a little change in you!"

What do you call a man who rescues drowning phantoms
from the sea?
A Ghost Guard!

What did the teacher ghost say to the pupil?

"Don't spook until you are spooken to."

What should you do with a sick witch?

Take her to the witch doctor.

What sort of positions do spooks get hired to fill?

Dead end jobs!

What do trainee witches do at school?

Spelling tests.

What do you call daydreams about broomsticks,
black cats, and pointy hats?
Witchful thinking.

Where do ghosts do their homework?
In an exorcise book.

What's red, has horns, and travels at the speed of light?
A speed demon.

When is it unlucky to
see a black cat?
When you're
a mouse!

What kind of shoes
do witches wear in
the summer?
Open toad sandals!

Which wizard never goes
to the barber?
Hairy Potter.

What do you call a warlock who tries to stop fights?
A peacelock.

Why did the druid keep falling over?
He couldn't get the staff.

What do you call a wizard who's really good at golf?
Harry Putter.

What do demons pack for their picnics?
Deviled eggs.

Why did the witch put her broom in the wash?
She wanted a clean sweep.

Why are mermaids easy to weigh?
Because they have their own scales.

What does Medusa do on a
bad hair day?
She pays a visit to the
snake charmer.

Doctor, whenever I say "Abracadabra"
people disappear.
Doctor, doctor, where are you?

What do you call a female wizard?
Magic Wanda.

When do ghosts usually appear?
Just before somebody screams.

Knock, knock!
Who's there?
Al.
Al who?
Al huff and I'll puff and blow your house down!

Why did the gingerbread man go to the doctor?
Because he was feeling crummy.

When I grow up, I'd like to marry a ghost.
What would possess you to do that?

How did the Good Weather Wizard get his name?
He loved sunny spells.

How can you tell whether a leprechaun is enjoying himself?
He's Dublin over with laughter.

Why was Cinderella a terrible tennis player?
She kept running away from the ball.

What parting gift was the young werewolf given
when he left home?
A comb!

What's the definition of
"Deadline?"
A fence around a
graveyard!

How should you greet a ghost?
"How do you boo?"

What do you call a big, fat troll?
A wobblin' goblin.

What do you get if you cross a
skeleton and a garden spade?
Skullduggery!

What do you call a wizard
with a cold?
A blizzard.

What do you get if you cross a wizard with an iceberg?
A cold spell.

**Why did the ogre's mother knit him three socks
as a birthday present?**
Because he had grown another foot.

What did the giant police officer eat for lunch?
Beef burglars!

**Why did Jack Frost refuse
to get married?**
Because he got cold feet!

Who grants your wishes but smells of fishes?
The fairy cod-mother.

Why did the dragon breathe on the map of the Earth?
Because he wanted to set the world on fire.

What happened to the man who didn't pay the exorcist's bill on time?
He was repossessed.

What does a witch doctor ask his guests at the start of a meal?
Voodoo like to sit down?

What is a female elf called?
A shelf.

Did you hear about the magician who walked down the street and turned into a bookstore?

Where did the sorcerer go to withdraw a crystal ball from its vault?
To the fortune teller.

What happened to the witch with the gingerbread house?
She was eaten out of house and home!

What do you call a troll of average size?
Medi-ogre.

Which fairy-tale character has a black belt in kung fu?
The ninja bread man.

How do mind readers
greet each other?
"You're fine, how am I?"

Why do leprechauns make
such good secretaries?
Because they're good
at shorthand.

What do you call a
black cat that falls off
a broomstick?
A catastrophe!

Where do skeletons keep their money?
In a joint account!

Why was the musical wizard standing on the roof in a
thunderstorm?
He was conducting lightning.

How does Jack Frost get to work?
By icicle.

What nationality is Santa Claus?
North Polish.

Why do witches fly on broomsticks?
Because vacuum cleaners are too heavy.

What did the ghostly pianist play?
Haunting melodies!

Why do skeletons make great comedians?
They have funny bones!

What has hooves, a long horn,
and squirts jam at you?
A unicorn eating a donut.

What are baby witches called?
Halloweenies.

What is the difference between a witch and the letters C, A, S, T, and S?
One casts spells and the other spells "casts!"

What happens when you see twin witches?
You can't tell which witch is which?

What happened to the ogre who put his dentures in back to front?
He ate himself.

What game do young ogres play?
Corpse and robbers!